Loop -d-Loop Crochet

NOVEL, ELEGANT CROCHET DESIGNS

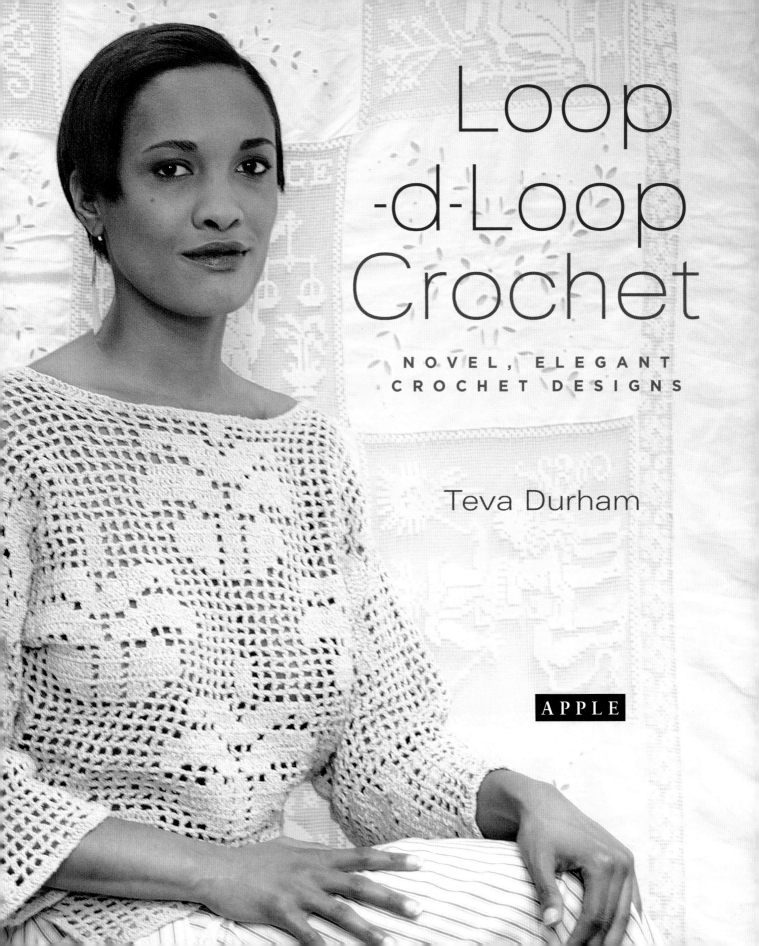

Loop
-d-Loop
Crochet

NOVEL, ELEGANT
CROCHET DESIGNS

Teva Durham

APPLE

To Margaret and Minerva,
and grandmothers everywhere whose love tempers the world.

First published in the UK in 2007 by
Apple Press
3rd Floor
7 Greenland Street
London
NW1 0ND
www.apple-press.com
ISBN: 978 1 84543 206 5

Edited by Melanie Falick

Book Design: Anna Christian
Production Manager: Anet Sirna-Bruder

First published in the United States of America in 2007 by Stewart, Tabori & Chang,
An imprint of Harry N. Abrams, Inc.
Text copyright © 2007 by Teva Durham
Photographs copyright © 2007 by Adrian Buckmaster
Pencil illustrations copyright © 2007 by Minerva Durham

The text of this book was composed in Gotham and Tribute.

Printed and bound in China
10 9 8 7 6 5 4 3 2 1

CONTENTS

INTRODUCTION

MANY PEOPLE REMARK THAT MY FIRST BOOK, *Loop-d-Loop: More Than 40 Novel Designs for Knitters*, is "not your grandma's" knitting book. These reviewers mean that the book, with its edgy designs, is suited to a new generation of crafters; plus, as fits this blogging age, it does not merely present pattern after pattern, but offers a gallery of images and personal introductions exploring the nature of creativity and fashion. This book is modeled after the first.

However, in many ways, this *is* my grandmas' crochet book. My own grandmothers were born in the first decade of the twentieth century, and they both died as I was just coming into adulthood. Working on this book was an opportunity for me to take an imaginary trip into their past. As I researched crochet patterns, it became clear that the development of many of these stitches stemmed from their era and the Victorian times that the elders in their childhood would've recalled. The beginning of the twentieth century was such an exciting time in literature, music, and art, as Impressionism ushered in Modernism and Romanticism yielded to the Jazz Age. While I sketched and swatched these designs, the lacy stitches lending themselves to a vintage feel, I caught a glimpse of that gilded age when life's pace, economics, and women's ingenuity often allowed for making complex garments in the home by hand. Crochet possesses an air of domesticity, having been a major component of the wedding trousseau. Looking at doilies, gloves, and tablecloths for inspiration, I found myself meditating upon the choices that were opening up to women in that era, and wondering about my own grandmothers' youthful ambitions. I felt incredibly blessed to be able to express myself through this medium of "woman's work."

I confess that for a long time, I was a knit snob who viewed crochet as a lesser craft, the poor stepsister to knitting. The backgrounds of my own grandmothers illustrate the roots of this prejudice. I was first taught to knit by my maternal grandmother, Minerva, whom we called Nani and who learned to knit in a tony convent school. I always believed I had inherited innate ability because of this stylish grandmother. I didn't know of any other talented crafters among my forebears, and certainly none as obsessed with fashion. On my father's side, a hillbilly aunt crocheted acrylic Santas, glued on googly eyes, backed them with magnets, and gave them out every year for Christmas; my dad now puts dozens on his refrigerator for kitschy holiday fun. However, on one recent visit to my father's house, I noticed a remarkable white cotton antimacassar on the back of a Queen Anne chair featuring two birds touching beaks on a ground of interlocking pineapple patterns. It looked like it belonged in a textile museum. I was surprised to learn that his mother, my grandmother Margaret, had crocheted this piece. I was unaware that Margaret, who had a sad upbringing as an orphan with a crippled leg, had interest or ability in any craft. In fact, I remember my parents laughing at Margaret's most prized possession—an electric organ with colour-coded keys and play-by-numbers songbooks—and her attempts to master it (Nani had been a classical pianist). Seeing Margaret's crochet work was a revelation.

Suddenly there was a flip side to my crafting heritage with which I wanted to get in touch. I, priding myself on being an expert knitter, was bowled over by the complexity of Margaret's crochet piece with its pattern so competently rendered. I wished she could have taught me how to manipulate a crochet hook around such a labyrinth. I studied the intricate pineapples and birds to understand how the rungs of chain stitch connected and formed the pictures. Accustomed to thinking as a knitter, in rows and stitches, I found something wonderful in the mysterious pathway the yarn took across motifs to build the pattern. By following the most logical track of the thread through the design, I could begin to break down the components to make sense of it as rows.

The discovery of this heirloom and the simultaneous influx of crochet fashions in boutiques and craft magazines excited me and compelled me to master crochet myself. Don't get me wrong; I had crocheted before this and even published a few patterns. But my challenge was to inhabit crochet to such an extent that I could create designs that had my stamp. I needed enough facility for my crochet designs to possess the same character as my knit designs—not to imitate my knitted fabric, but to exhibit the same signature qualities.

It was like free-falling into a new dimension at first. Holding one hook instead of two needles felt strange. As a practiced knitter, even an adventurous one, I was accustomed to forming fabric in a self-evident and solid way, often with both elbows braced on the armrests of my favorite chair. Crocheting seemed to divvy up the negative space along with the fabric; much of it amounted to skipping a certain number of chains. I began to enjoy this break from knitting and to contemplate where I could take crochet design-wise.

For those unfamiliar with *Loop-d-Loop*, I have a somewhat "outside-the-box" approach to design. But what first appears unorthodox is actually steeped in tradition—it takes old-fashioned techniques and styles out of context and into the hip-hop age. I try to create a tension of opposites within a design—rough-hewn yet delicate, stark yet feminine, organic yet structured, asymmetrical yet balanced. I love working garments circularly and utilizing other directional construction so that the process becomes self-evident in the product.

A switch to crochet can be a freeing experience for an avid knitter. As master knitting and crochet teacher Prudence Mapstone has discovered, crochet easily lends itself to freeform improvisation. The experience of crocheting is different: You don't hold all the stitches of a row on your needle at once but can more easily travel here and there over the building fabric. You are freed from thinking in horizontal (rows) and vertical (stitches). This modus operandi has a natural fit with my design sensibility. Often, I seek out this sort of mobility when knitting and use circular needles to go around a motif in imitation of crochet. Many of the shaping techniques that fascinate me in knitting, such as short rows, are actually a more natural move in crochet—you don't have to wrap stitches, just turn! In addition, three-dimensional and lace effects are easier to compose with a hook. Medallions created by knitting in counterpanes can be complicated, involving double-pointed needles and lots of calculated increasing, whereas crocheted medallions are comparatively easy—you can just keep crocheting around, building outward as you go. Moreover, knitted lace is different in character than crocheted lace, which is a closer imitation of vintage bobbin laces. And this vintage feel is why crochet is making such a fashion comeback.

After exploring crochet in depth, I have an equal love and respect for it and knitting. Some of my knit-blogging friends will have fits of the vapors upon reading this. Yet, still more are simultaneously joining the crochet cognoscenti in droves. I hope my perspective will be enjoyed by knitters who are delving into crochet as well as by crafters for whom crochet is their forte.

Teva

Half-Double, Double, Triple and Double-Triple

HALF-DOUBLE, DOUBLE, TRIPLE, AND DOUBLE-TRIPLE

THE BASIC CROCHET STITCHES—DOUBLE, HALF-DOUBLE, TRIPLE, double-triple, and so on—consist of various numbers of loops formed and pulled through one another until the hook is holding only one loop again. The result is a series of stitches uniformly increasing in height: The more loops you pull through, the taller the stitch created. From a knit design perspective, I found it exciting to work with a set of stitches tantamount to building blocks. With the standard repertoire of knit stitches, it is complex to build fabric vertically at different rates. For instance, a sloped shoulder involves several shaping rows in knitting, while it's accomplished with only a single row of short-to-tall stitches in crochet. This newfound facility to build with crochet was a revelation, and I enjoyed making use of the possibilities.

Admittedly, crochet fabric has some qualities that seem disadvantageous when designing garments. In crochet, unlike knitting, the yarn loops don't sit on a flat plane but are doubled upon themselves, leading to a stiffer, thicker, and often heavier fabric. And any stitch taller than a half-double crochet will not provide a solid fabric but will have slits of space between each stitch. Yet, as I worked up swatches and samples for this book, I often tenderly admired the simple, rustic beauty of the basic crochet stitches. Rows of ridged texture appear like furrows in a field ready to plant or like straw on a thatched roof, calling to mind a bucolic landscape, restful in a modern, media-frenzied world. I've selected yarns for this chapter in this mood; among them are dry, fibrous, plant-based yarns such as linen and bamboo and a rough-hewn, yet luxurious, silk-blend tweed.

Here I present five projects that highlight the characteristics of the basic crochet stitches: A wide belt in double crochet and ankle boots in half-treble crochet utilize the firm fabric perfect for structured accessories, while a basic tunic flaunts a textural striping of more compact and longer stitches. I also explore different possibilities in construction: The Hip-Slung Belt features partial-row shaping, the Brocade Boots use both rows and rounds, the Patch Pocket Skirt is done in mock rounds of wrong-side and right-side rows, and the back of the Girl's Bolero is worked circularly from its centre out in a spiral.

hip-slung belt

Wide belts, some remin-
iscent of geisha-like
obis, Zorro-like cummer-
bunds, Caribbean pirate
sashes, or their heroines'
corsets, perennially
become the must-have
item of the season, often
in association with a
blockbuster film. Even if
they are a fashion fetish
driven by Hollywood,
they are a natural pairing
with both chic bohemian
skirts and sleek dresses.
I've designed mine to
be more of an art piece,
a statement immune to
fashion's whims.

>> See pattern on page 20.

brocade boots

These boots call to mind a memory from the Burbank Ramada Inn. I'm immersed in a bubbling hot tub surrounded by mirrors, the shag carpet is strewn with yarn, and on the TV is what's tantamount to knitter's porn: an attractive woman (knitter Tina Marrin) taking a power drill to a kitten-heeled pump. It was the night before my stint as a guest on DIY Network's *Knitty Gritty*, and the producer had asked me to review a few episodes in preparation. While I hurriedly made more "step-outs" of my project by working samples up to various points, jumping into the hot tub to revive myself, I made a study of Tina's demonstration. She drilled holes around the base of the pumps, pulled loops through them with a crochet hook, and proceeded to knit boots. I'm a sissy when it comes to power tools, but this inspired me to figure out my own way to use an existing shoe as a base for boots. Here, fabric covers a rubber wedge sole, providing the foundation from which to crochet the boot. I've given these ankle boots an Edwardian look with brocade fabric in ochre hues, but I think they'd also be fabulous in a primary colour and pleather for a Mod look.

>> *See pattern on page 22.*

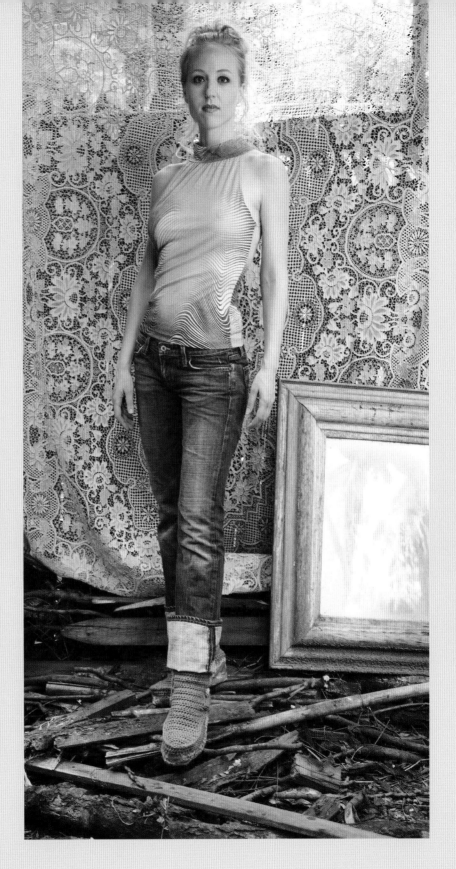

patch pocket skirt

When I was a girl, my mom was into wrap skirts big time. They were a convenient uniform for a young bohemian mother fresh out of art school, one who found herself trapped, for want of a starter house, in the conservative neighborhood in which she had grown up. I have vivid memories of pressing myself into those skirts out of shyness at many a patio party. As soon as my dad got a college teaching position, Mom demanded the luxury of ordering clothes from mail-order catalogs that featured preppy housewives in resort and leisure wear. I loved leafing through the pages of her Lilly Pulitzer and Marimekko catalogs, where there were sometimes mother-daughter versions of her wrap skirts, and I begged her to get us a matching set. I don't recall if she ever indulged me; as with many things, the yearning felt better than actual possession. What I do remember is spending many hours drawing my own versions of these catalogs. I was six then, but I swear my sketches resemble what I design today.

>> See pattern on page 24.

girl's bolero

The Fall 2005 cover of *Vogue Knitting* featured a knit bolero by designer Annie Modesitt, worked outward from centre back in a giant circle. That folksy-chic garment evoked braided rag rugs and intrigued knitters with its construction: Its rounded front lapels are the outer rims of the same circle. My little bolero jacket begins at centre back with a crocheted circle much like one that would make up a granny-square afghan.

If pressed to choose a favorite basic crochet stitch for a garment, half-treble, as here, wins my vote. Half-treble is longer and more relaxed than double crochet. The extra yarn over loop, that is made but not pulled through, creates an extra little flourish as it rests diagonally at the top of each stitch, extending the row height without the rigidity or grid-like openness of treble crochet.

>> See pattern on page 27.

track stitch tunics

Track stitch derives its name from railroad tracks—its basic unit consists of long vertical "ties" of treble-triple stitches bordered by a set of double crochet "rails." For these casual tunics I played with the textural striping. Seemingly random, somewhat asymmetrical stripes are a favorite ploy of mine. I find it exciting to arrange a sequence that makes the eye scramble to find balance in what at first appears arbitrary. Rather than striving for exacting, precise, and almost mechanized patterning, I try to re-create the organic order and proportion found in nature. There is a trick to this that artists have been using for centuries: the Fibonacci sequence, in which each number in the series is derived by adding together the previous two (1, 2, 3, 5, 8, and so on). A harmony is created by juxtaposing these numbers in the proportions of stripes. In this tunic, you can follow my sequence precisely or improvise your own rendition.

>> See pattern on page 31.

hip-slung belt

MEASUREMENTS
To fit high hips: 86.4 (96.5, 106.7, 116.8, 127) cm

Should fit slung snug on hips with 5.1 cm overlap

Shown in smallest size

YARN
Louet Sales "Euroflax Originals" (100% linen), sport weight yarn

2 (2, 3, 3, 4) hanks (3.5 oz/ 100 g; 270 yd/247 m) in #2014 champagne

HOOKS
3.75 mm (US F/5) or size to match gauge

NOTIONS
Horn Shaped Button (available at M&J Trimming)

3 (3, 4, 4, 4) metres braided leather cord

GAUGE
With 2 strands of yarn held together as one, 16 sts and 16 rows = 10.2 cm in dc

Always check and MATCH gauge for best results.

OVERVIEW
Belt is worked in rows of dc for its length beginning at rounded end. A wedge of partial rows at each back hip curve out the bottom edge.

LEFT FRONT
With 2 strands of yarn held together as one, work 13ch.

Row 1 (WS): Dc in 2nd ch from hook, dc in each ch across, turn—12 dc.

Row 2: 1ch, 2 dc in first dc, dc in each st across, turn—13 dc.

Rows 3–11: Rep Row 2—22 dc at end of last rnd.

Rows 12–17: 1ch, dc in each dc across, turn—22 dc.

Row 18 (RS): *Note: the beg of RS row will be the bottom edge of belt and end of RS row is top edge.* 1ch, dc in first dc, dc2tog worked across next 2 sts, dc in each st across, turn—21 dc.

Row 19 (WS): 1ch, dc in each st across to within last 2 sts, dc2tog worked across last 2 sts, turn—20 sts.

Rows 20–23: Rep Rows 18–19 twice—16 sts at end of last row.

Row 24: 1ch, dc in first dc, dc2tog worked across next 2 sts, dc in each dc across to last st, 2 dc in last st, turn—16 sts. *(Note: stitch number not altered, but belt tilted up towards top edge.)*

Row 25: 1ch, 2 dc in first st, dc in each st across to within last 2 sts, dc2tog worked across last 2 dc, turn—16 sts.

Rows 26-29: Rep 24-25 (twice)—16 sts.

Row 30: 1ch, 2 dc in first dc, dc in each st across, turn—17 sts.

Row 31: 1ch, dc in each st across, turn—17 sts.

Row 32-35: Rep Rows 30–31 twice—19 sts.

Work even in dc until piece measures 30.5 (33, 35.6, 38.1, 40.6) cm from beg, ending with a WS row.

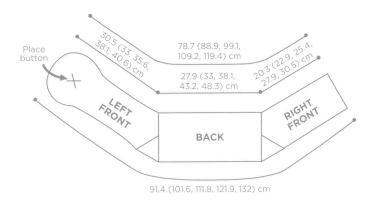

LEFT HIP GUSSET

Beg Partial Row Shaping Back Left Hip:

Row 1 (RS): 1ch, dc in each of first 10 dc, turn, leaving rem sts unworked—10 dc.

Row 2: 1ch, skip first dc, dc in each of next 9 dc, turn—9 dc.

Row 3: 1ch, dc in each dc across to within last dc, turn, leaving rem st unworked—8 dc.

Row 4: 1ch, skip first dc, dc in each dc across, turn—7 dc.

Rows 5-10: Rep Rows 3–4 (3 times)—1 dc at end of last row.

BACK

Row 1 (RS): 1ch, working across partial row shaping of Hip Gusset, dc in each row-end st, working across top edge of last row of Front, dc in each of next 9 sts, turn—19 dc.

Work even on 19 dc until top (shorter) edge measures 27.9 (33, 38.1, 43.2, 48.3) cm from beg of Back, ending with a WS row.

RIGHT HIP GUSSET

Beg Partial Row Shaping Back Right Hip:

Row 1 (RS): 1ch, dc in each of first 2 dc, slip st in next st, turn—2 dc.

Row 2: Dc in first sl st, dc in each dc across, turn—3 dc.

Row 3: 1ch, dc in each dc across previous row, dc in next dc on last row of Back, sl st in next dc, turn—4 dc.

Rows 4-7: Rep Rows 2–3 (twice)—8 dc at end of last row.

Row 8: Rep Row 2—9 dc.

RIGHT FRONT

Row 1 (RS): 1ch, dc in each of next 9 dc of Hip Gusset, dc in each remaining dc across last row of Back—19 dc.

Work even on 19 dc until piece measure 20.3 (22.9, 25.4, 27.9, 30.5) cm from beg of Right Front.

FINISHING

Edging: 1ch, dc evenly around entire outer edge of Belt, sl st in first dc to join. Fasten off.

Attach Toggle Button to centre of rounded end of belt (Left Front), using small length of leather cord through holes of button (or button post) and tying securely on WS. Mark centre of belt 15.2 (17.8, 20.3, 22.9, 25.4) cm from Right Front edge. Fold remaining length of leather cord in half and working from WS thread each end up through to RS of fabric 1.3 cm above and below centre line of belt. To secure belt, wrap around hips with rounded end extending from left hip past centre front of body, overlapping straight end and cords at right hip. Holding the two cord ends together, wrap them forward and around the toggle and then bring them back to right hip and around back and left hip. Tie ends to base of toggle to secure.

brocade boots

OVERVIEW
Boot is constructed in two pieces: Stitches are picked up all around sole constructed of fabric over a rubber wedge base, then a tongue piece is incorporated to form front of shoe, and back ankle is shaped.

TOP FRONT OF BOOT/ TONGUE PIECE (make 2)

Starting at toe, with 2 strands of yarn held together, make 10ch.

Row 1: Htr in 3rd ch from hook, htr in each ch across, turn—8 sts.

Shape Toe: Row 2: 2ch (does not count as a st), 2 htr in first htr, htr in each htr across to last htr, 2 htr in last htr, skip t-ch, turn—10 sts.

Row 3: Rep Row 2—12 sts.

Row 4: 2ch (does not count as a st), htr in each st across, turn—12 sts.

Work even in htr until piece measures 7.6 (8.9, 10.2) cm from beg.

Shape Top/Arch of Foot: Rows 1–4: Rep Row 2—20 sts at end of last row.

Row 5: 2ch (counts as htr), htr in each st across, turn—20 sts.

Decrease for Ankle: Row 6: Sl st in first 2 sts, 2ch (counts as htr), htr in each of next 17, turn, leaving remaining st unworked—18 sts.

Row 7: 2ch htr in each st across, turn—18 sts.

Work even in htr until piece measures 14.6 cm from beg of Decrease for Ankle.

Woman's shoe sizes 2 1/2–3 1/2 (4 1/2–5 1/2, 6 1/2–7 1/2)
Shown in largest size

MEASUREMENTS
Base is 21.6–22.9 (22.9–24.1, 25.4–26.7) cm long measured straight from toe to heel.

YARN
Rowan "Wool Cotton" (50% merino /50% cotton), light worsted weight yarn
3 (4, 4) balls (1.75 oz/ 50 g; 123 yd/113 m) in #964 still

HOOKS
3.75 mm (US F/5) or size to match gauge
Steel hook 2.75 mm (size 1)

NOTIONS
1 pair rubber "wedgie" flip flops, available at pharmacies and large retail chains; those shown are Old Navy 301508

1 pair unisex (better for width) cut-to-fit foam insoles, such as Dr. Scholls

1 metre cotton brocade, tapestry or other woven upholstery fabric

X-acto knife or sharp scissors

Sharp upholstery needle

Strong thread to match fabric

Covered Button Kit (Prym Dritz size #36) for 2.5 cm diameter metal shaft buttons

GAUGE
With larger hook and 2 strands of yarn held together as one, 16 sts and 12 rows = 10.2 cm in htr

Always check and MATCH gauge for best results.

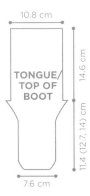

TONGUE/
TOP OF
BOOT

10.8 cm

14.6 cm

11.4 (12.7, 14) cm

7.6 cm

PREPARE WEDGIE FOR BASE

Cut rubber thong piece off flip-flop trimming as close to base as possible. Place foam insole along top sole and cut to match shape. Place each wedgie sole down on fabric aligning straight with grain and trace outline onto fabric. Cut, leaving 1.6 cm seam allowance. Cut a strip (perpendicular to grain of fabric; on the fabric's cross-grain) long enough to wrap around sides of entire sole plus extra 5.1 cm (for seam allowance each edge) and 5.1 cm taller than highest part of wedge. Beg at 12.7 cm from centre back heel measured around curve of wedge, at inner arch of sole, leaving 1.6 cm seam allowance, sew strip along each sole piece with RS pressed together, easing around curves so strip is perpendicular to sole. Fit wedgie in covering and make adjustments to line of seam if necessary. Trim excess seam allowance. Sew 2 ends of strip together and trim excess seam allowance. Trim top of strip so it extends 2.5 cm above wedgie all around. Fold top of strip to WS so 1.9 cm is folded toward inside and folded edge is 6 mm above top of wedge. Thread sharp upholstery needle with 1 strand yarn and working through doubled fabric, beg at seam of strip, work a row of running stitches (approx 4 sts over 2.5 cm including each st at front and back of fabric—needle up, down, up, down), 3 mm below top of fabric all around.

LEFT BOOT

Work Base of Boot: Foundation Rnd: Using smaller hook, join single strand of yarn in one running st at seam of strip (on arch side of boot), 1ch, work dc in 82 (86, 90) running sts, working in all sts on RS of fabric and skipping or working in sts on WS of fabric as necessary to equalize distance between sts as foll: work 36 dc evenly spaced from starting place around heel to opposite side of sole (to place approx 12.7 cm from centre back heel—25.4 cm around curve of heel), then work 46 (50, 54) sts evenly spaced around front of shoe to beg, sl st in first dc to join—82 (86, 90) sts made.

Rnd 1: With larger hook, join second strand of yarn, and with yarn doubled, 2ch, htr in each dc around, sl st in 2ch to join—82 (86, 90) sts made.

Rnd 2: 2ch, htr in each htr around, sl st in t-ch to join—82 (86, 90) sts made.

Rnd 3 (joining rnd): 2ch (counts as htr), htr in each of first 36 htr, take up Foot/Tongue piece and beg at edge of Ankle Decrease row (called Row 6), with WS of Base and Foot pieces together, with Base facing you, working through double thickness, *insert hook in next st of Base from RS to WS and then through side edge of Foot/Tongue piece from WS to RS in one motion, draw up a loop, yo, draw yarn through both loops on hook (dc made through both pieces at once); rep from * distributing top piece equally around 46 (50, 54) sts of shoe front, sl st in 2ch to join. Do not fasten off.

HEEL/BACK OF BOOT

Back of Boot is now worked in rows.

Row 1 (RS): 2ch, htr in each of next 35 htr around heel to junction of Top Front, turn—36 sts.

Row 2 (WS): 2ch, htr in each st across, turn—36 sts.

Shape Back Ankle: Row 3 (decrease): 2ch, htr in each of next 13 htr, (hdc2tog over next 2 sts) 4 times, htr in each of last 14 sts, turn—32 sts.

Rows 4–7: 2ch (counts as htr), htr in each st across, turn—32 sts.

Row 8 (decrease): 2ch, hdc2tog over next 2 sts, htr in each st across to last 2 sts, hdc2tog over last 2 sts, turn—30 sts.

Work even in htr until back of boot measures 14 cm from where picked up from fabric (should be 6 mm shorter than Front/Tongue piece). Do not fasten off.

Edging: Working down side edge of Back of Boot, work 2 dc in each row-end htr down to junction of Foot/Tongue, 2 dc in each row-end st up side edge of Tongue, dc in each st across top of Tongue, 2 dc in each row-end st down other side edge of Tongue to junction, 2 dc in each row-end st up other side edge of Back, dc in each st across top edge of Back, sl st in first dc to join. Fasten off.

FINISHING

At inner arch of boot: Overlap Front/Tongue piece on top of Back piece edges by 6 mm (top of front piece extends 6 mm higher) and sew with 1 strand of yarn and upholstery needle, leaving 1.9 cm of back piece free at top and 2.5 cm of front piece free.

Make covered buttons out of fabric following kit directions.

Sew buttons: At outer edge of boot: Sew first button 4.5 cm in from side and top edges of back boot piece, sew another button 5.1 cm down from first and 3.8 cm in from edge.

Button loops: Make first 5.1 cm down from top of Front/Tongue piece as follows: With 2 strands yarn and larger hook, sl st in edge, 4ch, sl st 2.5 cm below joining, turn, work 6 dc in 4ch loop to cover, secure yarn and fasten off. Make another button loop beg 2.5 cm below bottom of first loop.

RIGHT BOOT

Work same as Left Boot, reversing shaping by beg at outside edge of boot opposite seam on inner arch.

patch pocket skirt

OVERVIEW

Skirt is worked from top down in the round alternating between RS and WS rounds in order to keep "seams" from spiraling. Then a separate piece is worked in rows and attached at right "seam" to overlap to resemble wrap skirt. Elastic at top provides better fit, but be sure to work foundation chain loosely—after joining foundation chain, have intended wearer step into it and make sure that it can be pulled over hips. A-line side "seam" shaping and back dart increases are done with aid of hanging stitch markers, place marker (pm)—place a marker by hanging on work between stitches, slip marker (slm)— rehang marker in same spot on subsequent rows as you work.

SKIRT

With MC, work {136 (148, 160, 172)}; 184 (200, 216, 232, 248) ch, join to first ch with slip st. Pm for right hip side "seam," turn.

Rnd 1 (WS): 3ch (counts as tr), skip first ch, tr in each of next {19 (21, 23, 25)}; 27 (29, 31, 33, 36) ch sts, pm for first back dart, tr in each of next {28 (30, 32, 34)}; 36 (40, 44, 48, 50) ch sts, pm for next back dart, tr in each of next {20 (22, 24, 26)}; 28 (30, 32,

---

Girl's sizes appear in fancy brackets; women's sizes appear after semicolon, where only one term is given it applies to all sizes.

Shown in girl's 12 and women's medium

MEASUREMENTS

To fit {girl's 8 (10, 12, 14)}; woman's S (M, L, XL, XXL)

High hip/low waist circumference: {57.2 (62.2, 67.3, 72.4) cm}; 77.5 (85.1, 91.4, 97.8, 105.4) cm before adding elastic

Hem circumference: {80 (85.1, 90.2, 95.3) cm}; 113 (119.4, 121.9, 133.4, 139.7) cm

Length: {38.1 (43.2, 48.3, 53.3) cm}; 63.5 cm

YARN

South West Trading Company "Bamboo" (100% bamboo fiber), sport weight yarn

For child's skirt: 4 (4, 5, 5) balls in (3.5 oz/100 g; 250 yd/228 m) lilac (MC), 1 ball plum (CC)

For women's skirt: 6 (7, 8, 9, 9) balls in jade (MC), 1 ball in lilac (CC)

HOOKS

2.75 mm (US C/2) or size to match gauge

NOTIONS

Hanging stitch markers

Elastic 2.5 cm wide to fit around low waist plus 1.6 cm for overlap

Sewing needle and matching sewing thread to sew in zipper

O Ring Buckles 3.8 cm

17.8 cm long Zipper to match MC.

GAUGE

24 sts and 12 rows = 10.2 cm in tr

Always check and MATCH gauge for best results.

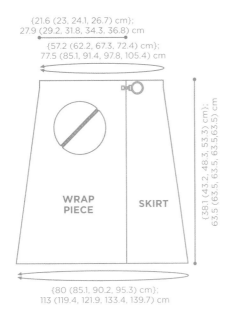

{21.6 (23, 24.1, 26.7) cm};
27.9 (29.2, 31.8, 34.3, 36.8) cm

{57.2 (62.2, 67.3, 72.4) cm};
77.5 (85.1, 91.4, 97.8, 105.4) cm

WRAP PIECE

SKIRT

{38.1 (43.2, 48.3, 53.3) cm};
63.5 (63.5, 63.5, 63.5, 63.5) cm

{80 (85.1, 90.2, 95.3) cm};
113 (119.4, 121.9, 133.4, 139.7) cm

34, 37) ch sts, pm for left hip side "seam," tr in each of next {68 (74, 80, 86)}; 92 (100, 108, 116, 124), sl st in t-ch to join, turn—{136 (148, 160, 172)}; 184 (200, 216, 232, 248) sts.

Rnd 2 (RS) (Back Dart Increase Rnd): 3ch (counts as tr), skip first st, tr in each tr across to first side marker, slm for side "seam," tr in each tr across to next back dart marker, slm for back dart, 2 tr in next st for inc, tr in each tr across to 1 st before next dart marker, 2 tr in next st, slm for back dart (this marker comes after the increase rather than before), tr in each tr across, sl st in t-ch to join, slm for side "seam," turn—{138 (150, 162, 174)}; 186 (202, 218, 234, 250) sts.

Rnd 3: 3ch (counts as tr), skip first st, tr in each st around, rehanging markers directly above, sl st in t-ch to join, turn—{138 (150, 162, 174)}; 186 (202, 218, 234, 250) sts.

Rnd 4 (Side "Seam" and Back Dart Increase Rnd): 3ch (counts as tr), tr in first st at base of t-ch for inc, tr in each tr across to 1 st before next side marker, 2 tr in next st, slm for side "seam," 2 tr in next st, tr in each tr across to next dart marker, slm for back dart, 2 tr in next st, tr in each tr across to 1 st before next dart marker, 2 tr in next st, slm for next back dart (this marker comes after the increase rather than before), tr in each tr across to last st, 2 tr in last st of rnd to inc, sl st in t-ch to join, slm for side "seam," turn—{144 (156, 168, 180)}; 192 (208, 224, 240, 256) sts.

Rnd 5: Rep Rnd 3—{144 (156, 168, 180)}; 192 (208, 224, 240, 256) sts.

Rnd 6 (Back Dart Increase Rnd): Rep Rnd 2—{146 (158, 170, 182)}; 194 (210, 226, 242, 258) sts.

Rnd 7: Rep Rnd 3—{146 (158, 170, 182)} sts.

Rnd 8 (Side "Seam" and Back Dart Increase Rnd): Rep Rnd 4—{152 (164, 176, 188)}; 200 (216, 232, 248, 264) sts.

Girls' Sizes Only: Rnds 9–11: Rep Rnd 3—{152 (164, 176, 188)}; 200 (216, 232, 248, 264) sts.

Women's Sizes Only: Rnd 9: Rep Rnd 3—200 (216, 232, 248, 264) sts.

Rnd 10 (Back Dart Increase Rnd): Rep Rnd 2—202 (218, 234, 250, 266) sts.

Rnd 11: Rep Rnd 3—202 (218, 234, 250, 266) sts.

All Sizes: Back dart increases complete. Remove back dart markers.

Rnd 12: 3ch (counts as tr), tr in first st at base of t-ch for inc, tr in each tr across to 1 st before next side marker, 2 tr in next st, slm for side "seam," 2 tr in next st, tr in each tr across to last st, 2 tr in last st of rnd to inc, slm for side "seam," sl st in t-ch to join, turn—{156 (168, 180, 192)}; 206 (222, 238, 254, 270) sts.

Women's Sizes Only: Work in est pattern, inc 2 tr at each side "seam" marker every 4th rnd 15 times—266 (282, 298, 314, 330) sts at end of last rnd.

Child's Sizes Only: Work in est pattern, inc 2 tr at each side "seam" marker every 4th rnd {8 (1, 1, 1)}; then work side "seam" incs every 5th rnd {0 (7, 1, 0)} times; then work side "seam" inc's every 6th row {0 (0, 6, 7)} times—{188 (200, 212, 224)} at end of last rnd.

All Sizes: Work even in tr until Skirt measures {38.1 (43.2, 48.3, 53.3) cm}; 63.5 cm from beg or desired length. Fasten off.

Bottom Edging: With RS facing, working across opposite side of foundation ch, join CC in first ch at right side "seam," 1ch, working from left to right, rev dc in each st around, sl st in first rev dc to join. Fasten off.

WRAP PIECE
Starting at top edge, with MC, work {52 (56, 60, 64)}; 67 (72, 77, 83, 89) ch.

Row 1 (WS): Tr into 4th ch on hook, tr into each ch across—{50 (54, 58, 62)}; 65 (70, 75, 81, 87) sts. Mark end of Row 1 as side edge.

Rows 2-3: 3ch (t-ch counts as tr), tr into each st across, turn—{50 (54, 58, 62)}; 65 (70, 75, 81, 87) sts.

Row 4 (Increase Row): 3ch (t-ch counts as tr), tr in first st at base of t-ch for inc, tr in each tr across, turn—{51 (55, 59, 63)}; 66 (71, 76, 82, 88) sts.

Women's Sizes Only: Work in established pattern, inc 1 st at side edge of every 4th row 17 times—83 (88, 93, 99, 105) sts.

Child's Sizes Only: Work in established pattern, inc 1 st at side edge of every 4th row {10 (3, 3, 3)} times; then inc 1 st at side edge of every 5th row {0 (7, 1, 0)} times; then inc 1 st at side edge of every 6th row {0 (0, 6, 7)} times—{61 (65, 69, 73)} sts at end of last row.

All Sizes: Work even in tr until Wrap Piece measures {38.1 (43.2, 48.3, 53.3) cm}; 63.5 cm from beg or desired length. Fasten off.

Edging: Row 1: With RS facing, join MC at bottom right-hand corner of Wrap Piece, 1ch, dc evenly across outer (straight) edge of Wrap Piece, working approximately 3 sts for every 2 rows. Fasten off.

Row 2: With RS facing, join CC at top left-hand corner of Wrap Piece, 1ch, working across opposite side of foundation ch, working from left to right, rev dc in each ch across top edge, 3 rev dc in corner st, rev dc in each dc down straight edge, 3 rev dc in corner st, rev dc in each st across bottom edge. Fasten off, leaving angled side edge unworked.

FINISHING
Pocket: Make 2 matching half circles, either in Straight Style as on woman's skirt or Bull's Eye style as on girl's skirt.

STRAIGHT STYLE POCKET HALF
(make 2)

With MC, work 47ch.

Row 1: Tr in 4th ch from hook, tr in each ch across, turn—45 sts.

Rows 2-4: 3ch (counts as tr), sk first tr, tr in each tr across, turn—45 sts.

Row 5: 3ch (counts as tr), sk first tr, (tr2tog in next 2 sts) twice, tr in each st across to within last 5 tr, (tr2tog in next 2 sts) twice, 1 tr in top of tch, turn—41 sts.

Rows 6-11: Rep Row 5—17 sts at end of last row. Fasten off.

BULL'S EYE POCKET HALF
(make 2)

With MC, work 4ch.

Row 1 (WS): 4 tr in 4th ch from hook, turn—5 sts.

Row 2: 3ch (counts as tr), tr into first tr, 2 tr in each tr across, turn—10 sts.

Row 3: 3ch (counts as tr), tr into first tr, 2 tr in next tr, *tr in next tr, 2 tr in next tr; rep from * across, turn—16 sts.

Row 4: 3ch (counts as tr), tr into first tr, tr in next tr, 2 tr in next tr, *tr in each of next 2 tr, 2 tr in next tr; rep from * across to t-ch, tr in top of t-ch, turn to work across bottom edge of half circle—22 sts.

Row 5: Dc evenly across bottom edge of circle half. Fasten off.

BOTH STYLES
Edging: With RS facing, join CC in last st on left side of curved edge of Pocket Half, 1ch, rev dc evenly across curved edge of Pocket Half. Fasten off. Rep Edging on other Half.

ASSEMBLY
Align pocket pieces into a circle and baste zipper along straight edges on WS of pieces. Sew zipper securely. Place pocket on Wrap Piece with zipper pull at top right and positioned at a 45 degree angle as shown. Sew Pocket to Skirt with yarn needle and MC working in small running stitch just inside of CC trim.

CASING
Try Skirt on intended wearer and mark low waist/high hip. Drape elastic tightly but comfortably around body at this point and cut elastic with 1.6 cm extra for overlap. Sew elastic to itself overlapping seam allowance. Hold elastic on WS of Skirt waist. With MC and crochet hook, with WS of Skirt waist facing work join MC in first ch of foundation ch, 1ch, *dc in foundation ch, pull up a loop approximately 2.5 cm long to cover elastic, dc in WS of corresponding st on Skirt below elastic, pull up a loop approximately 2.5 cm long, skip 2 ch on foundation ch edge, dc in next ch; rep from * around waist, sl st in first dc to join. Fasten off.

With WS of Wrap Piece aligned over RS of skirt, match angled edge along side "seam." Pin edge from waist to bottom hem. Use hook and MC to slip st the edge of Wrap Piece to Skirt. With MC sew O ring buckle to Skirt opposite Wrap piece.

INTERMEDIATE

girl's bolero

To fit child's size 4–5 (6–7, 8–9)
Shown in smallest size

MEASUREMENTS
Chest: 61 (68.6, 77.5) cm closed
Back length: 38.1 (41.9, 47) cm

YARN
Crystal Palace "Iceland" (100% wool) bulky singles yarn
2 (2, 3) balls (3.5 oz/ 100 g; 109 yd/100 m) each in #8166 sienna (A); #1219 fuchsia (B); and #9719 claret (C)

HOOKS
10 mm (US N/15) or size to match gauge

NOTIONS
Yarn needle
1 m ribbon (ribbon shown is 2.5 cm satin backed velvet)

GAUGE
First 3 rnds of Back = 12.7 cm in diameter. 7 sts and 5 rows = 10.2 cm in htr
Always check and MATCH gauge for best results.

OVERVIEW
The back of Bolero is worked in a circle in spiraling rounds alternating colors each round—colour changes will show spiraling shift of stripes (beg of each rnd appears to be 1 rnd before end of round) and this junction will be placed at centre bottom. Back hem is done in rows of interlocked stripes to match. Each front is a half-circle. Sleeves are worked lengthwise with bell cuff added along one edge. *[Note: All rnds/rows are worked from RS for consistent textured striping, however, you can assemble with either side showing as long as all pieces match. I like the braided rug look of the WS of fabric to show rather than the smoother RS.]* To change colour, complete last st with first colour, draw loop of next colour through loop on hook (ch made), then cut first colour leaving small length to weave in later.

BACK
With A, 2ch, join with sl st to form centre ring.

Rnd 1: 2ch, 5 htr in centre ring—6 sts. Do not join. Work in a spiral.

Rnd 2: 2 htr in 2ch t-ch, 2 htr in each of next 5 htr—12 sts.

Rnd 3: Change to B, 2 htr in each htr around—24 sts.

Rnd 4: Change to C, 2 htr in each htr around—48 sts.

Rnd 5: Change to A, htr in each htr around—48 sts.

Rnd 6: Change to B, htr in each htr around—48 sts.

Smallest Size Only: Square off the side and top edges of circle to shape Back shoulders/neck beg next rnd over 3 rnds as foll:

Rnd 7: Change to C, htr in each of next 9 htr, dc in each of next 2 htr, sl st in each of next 4 htr, dc in each of next 2 htr, htr in each of next 5 htr, sl st in each of next 4 htr (place a marker between 2nd and 3rd sl st to mark centre back neck), htr in each of next 5 htr, dc in each of next 2 htr, sl st in each of next 4 htr, dc in each of next 2 htr, htr in each of next 9 htr—48 sts.

Rnd 8: Change to A, htr in each of next 9 htr, sl st in each of next 8 sts, 2 htr in each of next 4 htr, htr in next htr, sl st in each of next 4 htr (back neck), htr in next htr, 2 htr in each of next 4 htr, sl st in each of next 8 sts, htr in each of next 9 htr—8 sts increased; 56 sts.

Rnd 9: Change to B, 2 htr in each of next 8 htr, htr in next htr, sl st in each of next 10 sts, htr in each of next 6 htr, sl st in each of next 6 sts (centre back neck is between 3rd and 4th sts), htr next htr, sl st in each of next 10 sts, htr in next htr), 2 htr in each of next 2 htr (place marker in this spot for beg of Hem), 2 htr in each of next 7 htr—16 sts increased; 72 sts. Do not fasten off. Do not turn.

Equalize/level off rnd shift at centre Back hem as foll:

Rnd 9 Extension: Working from end of Rnd 9 at centre bottom Back to what will be side edge, change to C, htr in each of next 14 sts. Fasten off C. Do not turn.

Smallest Size Hem: Work now progresses in Rows.

Row 10: With RS facing, join C in marked htr in Rnd 9 (28 before end of Rnd 9 Extension), 2ch (counts as htr), htr in each of next 13 sts, change to A, htr in each of next 14 sts—28 sts. Fasten off A. Do not turn.

Row 11: With RS facing, join A in top of t-ch in Row 10, 2ch (counts as htr), htr in each of next 13 htr, change to B, htr in each of next 14 sts—28 sts. Fasten off B. Do not turn.

Row 12: With RS facing, join B in top of t-ch in Row 11, 2ch (counts as htr), htr in each of next 13 htr, change to C, htr in each of next 14 sts—28 sts. Fasten off C. Do not turn.

Second and Third Sizes: Rnd 7: Change to C, 2 htr in each htr around—96 sts.

Third Size Only: Rnd 8: Change to A, htr in each htr around—96 sts.

Second and Third Sizes Only: Square off the side and top edges of circle to shape Back shoulders/neck beg with next rnd, worked over 3 rnds as foll:

Rnd 8 (9): Change to A (B), htr in each of next 14 htr, dc in each of next 4 htr, sl st in each of next 14 (13) htr, dc in each of next 4 htr, htr in each of next 9 htr, sl st in each of next 6 (8) htr (place a marker between 3rd and 4th [4th and 5th] sl st to mark centre back neck), htr in each of next 9 htr, dc in each of next 4 htr, sl st in each of next 14 (13) htr, dc in each of next 4 htr, htr in each of next 14 htr—96 sts.

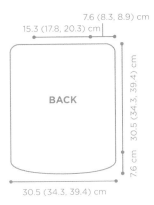

BACK

7.6 (8.3, 8.9) cm

15.3 (17.8, 20.3) cm

30.5 (34.3, 39.4) cm

7.6 cm

30.5 (34.3, 39.4) cm

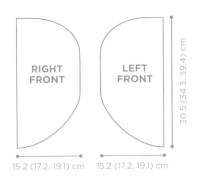

RIGHT FRONT

LEFT FRONT

30.5 (34.3, 39.4) cm

15.2 (17.2, 19.1) cm

15.2 (17.2, 19.1) cm

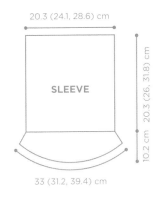

SLEEVE

20.3 (24.1, 28.6) cm

20.3 (26, 31.8) cm

10.2 cm

33 (31.2, 39.4) cm

Rnd 9 (10): Change to B (C), htr in each of next 14 htr, dc in each of next 2 sts, sl st in each of next 18 (17) sts, dc in each of next 2 sts, htr in each of next 4 sts, 2 htr in each of next 4 htr, htr in next htr, sl st in each of next 6 (8) htr (back neck), htr in next htr, 2 htr in each of next 4 htr, htr in each of next 4 sts, dc in each of next 2 sts, sl st in each of next 18 (17) sts, dc in each of next 2 sts, htr in next 14 htr—8 sts increased; 104 sts.

Rnd 10 (11): Change to C (A), 2 htr in each of next 12 (14) htr, htr in each of next 2 (0) htr, sl st in next 22 (21) sts, htr in each of next 12 htr, sl st in each of next 8 (10) sts (centre back neck is between 4th and 5th [5th and 6th] sts), htr in each of next 12 htr, sl st in each of next 22 (21) sts, dc in each of next 2 (0) htr, (place marker in next st for beg of Hem), 2 htr in each of next 12 (14) htr—24 (28) sts increased; 128 (132) sts. Do not turn.

Rnd 10 (11) Extension: Equalize/level off rnd shift at centre Back hem as foll: Working from end of Rnd 10 (11) centre bottom Back to what will be side edge, change to A (B), htr in next 24 (28) sts. Fasten off A (B). Do not turn.

Second and Third Sizes Hem: Work now progresses in rows.

Row 11 (12): With RS facing, join A (B) in marked htr in Rnd 10 (11) (52 [56] sts before end of Rnd 10 [11] Extension), 2ch, htr in each of next 25 (27) sts, change to B (C), htr in each of next 24 (28) sts—48 (56) sts. Fasten off B (C). Do not turn.

Row 12 (13): With RS facing, join B (C) in top of t-ch in last row, 2ch (counts as htr), htr in each of next 23 (27) htr, change to C (A), htr in each of next 24 (28) sts—48 (56) sts. Fasten off C (A).

Row 13 (14): With RS facing, join C (A) in top of t-ch in last row, 2ch (counts as htr), htr in each of next 23 (27) htr, change to A (B), htr in each of next 24 (28) sts—48 (56) sts. Fasten off A (B).

FIRST FRONT

(Becomes Left Front if you use WS of fabric, Right Front if you use RS of fabric. End of RS row is neck/shoulder.)

With A, 2ch, join with sl st in first ch.

Row 1: 2ch (counts as htr), 2 htr in ring, turn—3 sts. Do not join. Fasten off. *(Note: In forming half circle Fronts to match Back, do not turn work, but work all rows in same direction.)*

Row 2 (RS): With RS facing, rejoin A in top of t-ch in last row, 2ch (counts as htr), skip first htr, 2 htr in each of next 2 sts—5 sts. Fasten off.

Row 3: With RS facing, join B in top of t-ch in last row, 2ch, htr in first htr, 2 htr in each htr across—10 sts. Fasten off.

Row 4: With RS facing, join C in top of t-ch in last row, 2ch, htr in first st, 2 htr in each htr across—20 sts. Fasten off.

Row 5: With RS facing, join A in top of t-ch in last row, 2ch, htr in each htr across—20 sts. Fasten off.

Row 6: With RS facing, join B in top of t-ch in last row, 2ch, htr in each htr across—20 sts. Fasten off.

Row 7: With RS facing, join C in top of t-ch in last row, 2ch, htr in each htr across—20 sts. Fasten off.

Smallest Size Only: Shape Front Neck over next 2 rows. *(Note: Beg of RS row is bottom hem).*

Row 8: With RS facing, join A in top of t-ch in last row, 2ch, htr each of next 10 htr, dc in each of next 4 sts, 2 htr in each of next 5 htr—25 sts. Fasten off.

Row 9: With RS facing, join B in top of t-ch in last row, 2ch, 2 htr in each of next 10 htr, dc in each of next 5 sts, (place a marker for ribbon tie position), 2 htr in next st, htr in next 7 sts, 2 htr in last st—37 sts. Fasten off.

Second and Third Sizes Only: Row 8: With RS facing, join A in top of t-ch in last row, 2ch, htr in first st, 2 htr in each htr across—40 sts. Fasten off.

Third Size Only: Row 9: With RS facing, join B in top of t-ch in last row, htr in each htr across—40 sts. Fasten off.

Second and Third Sizes: Shape Front Neck over next 2 rows.

Row 9 (10): With RS facing, join B (C) in top of t-ch in last row, 2ch, htr in each of next 13 sts, dc in each of next

16 sts, 2 htr in each of next 10 htr—50 sts. Fasten off.

Row 10 (11): With RS facing, join C (A) in top of t-ch in last row, 2ch, htr in next 13 sts, dc in next 14 sts (place a marker for ribbon tie position), 2 htr in next dc, htr in next 20 sts, 1 (2) htr in last st—1 (2) increases made; 51 (52) sts. Fasten off.

SECOND FRONT

(Becomes Right Front if you use WS of fabric; Left Front if you use RS of fabric. Beg of RS row is neck/shoulder.)

Work same as First Front through Row 7 (8, 9).

Smallest Size Only: Shape Front Neck over next 2 rows. *(Note: Beg of RS row is bottom hem.)*

Row 8: With RS facing, join A in top of t-ch in last row, 2ch, htr first st, 2 htr in each of next 4 htr, dc in each of next 4 sts, htr in each of next 11 sts—25 sts. Fasten off.

Row 9: With RS facing, join B in top of t-ch in last row, 2ch, htr in first st, htr in each of next 7 sts, 2 htr in next st (place a marker for ribbon tie position), dc in each of next 5 sts, 2 htr in each of next 10 htr, htr in last st—37 sts. Fasten off.

Second and Third Sizes Only: Shape Front Neck over next 2 rows.

Row 9 (10): With RS facing, join B (C) in top of t-ch in last row, 2ch, htr in first st, 2 htr in each of next 9 htr, dc in each of next 16 sts, htr in each of next 14 sts—50 sts. Fasten off.

Row 10 (11): With RS facing, join C (A) in top of t-ch in last row, 2ch, work 0 (1) htr in first st, htr in next 20 sts, 2 htr in next st, (place a marker for ribbon tie position), dc in each of next 14 sts, htr in each of next 14 sts—1 (2) increases made; 51 (52) sts. Fasten off.

SLEEVE (make 2)

With A, ch 17 (20, 23).

Row 1: Htr in 3rd ch from hook, htr each ch across—16 (19, 22) sts. Fasten off.

Row 2 (RS): With RS facing, join B in top of t-ch in last row, 2ch, htr in each htr across—16 (19, 22) sts. Fasten off.

Rep Row 2 alternating colors in sequence, always working from RS, working a total of 10 (12, 14) rows.

FINISHING

Consider which side of fabric will be facing outward on all pieces and weave in yarn ends on WS. Arrange Fronts and Back with curved edge of Fronts pointed toward centre and neck shaping to top. Sew shoulder seams, leaving 10 (12, 14) centre back neck sts open and seaming [4 (12, 13) sts of each top Front to corresponding sts of Back. Sew side seams, leaving 5 (6, 7) rows of front open and matching portion of Back open for Sleeves (Back is slightly longer, but ease in, sewing all 3 rows of Back hem to side of each Front).

Attach Sleeve: Sew Sleeve seam, matching foundation ch to last row.

Position Sleeve so that stripes align with stripes of Fronts (Rows 1–5 [1–6, 1–7] stripe colors of Sleeve should align with top 5 [6, 7] rows of each front). Sew top of Sleeve around armhole on Front and Back.

SLEEVE CUFF

(Note: Work with RS facing [which if you chose like me is now at inside of sleeve].)

Find centre 2 Sleeve rows at cuff edge—between 5th/6th (6th/7th, 7th/8th) rows. Join A in the row-end st to the right of centre.

Row 1: 2ch (does not count as st), 2 htr in same row-end st, htr in base of next row, 2 htr in top of next row-end st—5 sts. Fasten off.

Row 2: With RS facing, join B in row-end st to the right of first st in Row 1, 2ch (counts as htr), 2 htr in same row-end st, 2 htr in each st across Row 1, 2 htr in next row-end st on Sleeve edge—17 sts. Fasten off.

Row 3: With RS facing, join C in 3rd (4th, 5th) row-end st on Sleeve edge to the right of first st in Row 2 (at seam), 2ch (counts as htr), htr in each row-end st across Sleeve edge, in each st across Row 2, and in each row-end st across rest of Cuff—23 (25, 27) sts. Fasten off.

Row 4: With RS facing, join A in in top of t-ch in last row, 2ch (counts as htr), htr in each htr across—23 (25, 27) sts. Fasten off.

Row 5: With RS facing, join B in in top of t-ch in last row, 2ch, htr in each st across—23 (25, 27) sts. Fasten off, leaving a sewing length to sew 3-row Cuff side seam. Sew Cuff seam.

NECK TRIM

With RS of Back neck facing (which may be facing the inside of sweater if you sewed it as I did), join B (C, A) (last colour in sequence for Front) in first st of Back neck edge, dc in each of next 10 (12, 14) sts across Back neck edge. Fasten off.

Insert ribbon through each Front at marked sts and tie.

track stitch tunic

OVERVIEW

Back and Front are each worked from hem up with varying sequence of track pattern, simple armhole shaping, and slit neck. Sleeves are done in two parts with the top piece worked from bicep up and sleeve bottom worked separately side to side.

BACK

With MC, work {45 (49, 53)}; 61 (67, 75, 81, 87) ch.

Foundation Row (WS): Dc in 2nd ch from hook, dc in each ch across, turn—{44 (48, 52)}; 60 (66, 74, 80, 86) dc.

Work Rows 1–10 of Track Stitch Pattern I {2}; 3 times; then work Rows 1–4 of Track Stitch Pattern II once; then work Rows 1–10 of Track Stitch Pattern I once; then work Rows 1–4 of Track Stitch Pattern II once, ending when measurements for desired size are reached. AT SAME TIME, when piece measures approx {25.4 (30.5, 30.5) cm}; 41.9 cm from beg, ending with any Row 2 of pattern, beg to shape armhole as follows.

Shape Armhole

Next Row: Sl st in first {3}; 4 (5, 6, 6, 6) sts, 1ch, dc in same st, dc in

Child's sizes appear in fancy brackets; adult sizes appear after semicolon, where only one term is given it applies to all sizes.
Shown in child's smallest two sizes and adult large

MEASUREMENTS
To fit {child 4–6 (8–10, 12–14)}; adult S (M, L, XL, XXL)
Finished Chest/Bust {68.6 (74.9, 81.3) cm}; 94 (102.9, 115.6, 124.5, 134.6) cm
Length {40.6 (48.3, 55.9) cm}; 63.5 (66, 68.6, 71.1, 73.7) cm

Sleeve length {34.3 (40.6, 45.7) cm}; 50.8 cm

YARN
Rowan "Summer Tweed" (70% silk; 30% cotton), worsted weight nubby yarn
Child's sweater: 5 (6, 7) hanks (1 3/4 oz/50 g; 118 yd/108 m): smallest size shown in #538 butterball yellow; medium size

shown in #524 cotton bud white
Adult sweater: 10 (11, 12, 13, 14) hanks (1 3/4 oz/ 50 g; 118 yd/108 m): shown in Large #515 in raffia

HOOK
3.5 mm (US E/4) or size needed to obtain gauge

NOTIONS
Yarn needle

GAUGE
13 sts = 10.2 cm and 10 rows = 11.4 cm in Track Stitch Pattern I
Always check and MATCH gauge for best results.

special stitches

TRACK STITCH PATTERN I

Foundation Row (WS): Dc in 2nd ch from hook, dc in each ch across, turn.

Row 1 (RS): 5ch (counts as trtr), skip first dc, trtr in each dc across, turn.

Row 2: 1ch, dc in each trtr across, dc in 5th ch of t-ch, turn

Rows 3–4: 1ch, dc in each dc across, turn.

Rows 5–8: Rep Rows 1–4.

Rows 9–10: Rep Rows 1–2.

Rep Rows 1–10 for Track Stitch Pattern I.

TRACK STITCH PATTERN II

Rows 1–4: Rep Rows 1–2 of Track Stitch Pattern I twice.

DC2TOG (decrease 1 double crochet)
(Insert hook in next st, yo, draw yarn through st) twice, yo, draw yarn through 3 loops on hook.

TTR2TOG (decrease 1 triple treble crochet)
(Yo 3 times, insert hook in next st, yo, draw yarn through st, yo, draw yarn through 2 loops on hook 3 times) twice, yo, draw yarn through 3 loops on hook.

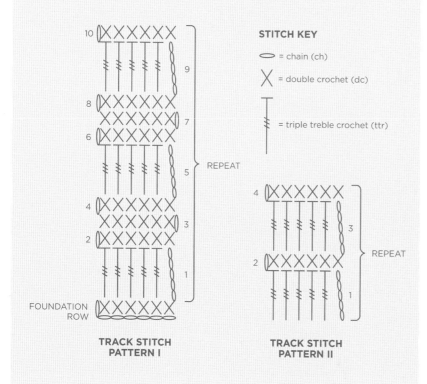

STITCH KEY

⬭ = chain (ch)

✕ = double crochet (dc)

‡ = triple treble crochet (ttr)

TRACK STITCH PATTERN I

TRACK STITCH PATTERN II

each st across to within last {2}; 3 (4, 5, 5, 5) sts, turn, leaving rem sts unworked—{40 (44, 48)}; 54 (58, 64, 70, 76) sts. Maintaining pattern, dec 1 st at each end of next 2 rows—{36 (40, 44)}; 50 (54, 60, 66, 68) sts. Work even in pattern until armhole measures {12.7 (15.2, 17.8) cm}; 19.1 (21.6, 24.1, 26.7, 29.2) cm, ending with a WS row (*Note: shoulder shaping adds 1.3 cm to armhole*).

Shape Shoulders/Back Neck

Next Row (RS): 2ch (counts as tr), skip first st, work {2 (3, 4)}; 4 (5, 6, 7, 7) tr, then work {3 (3, 4)}; 5 (5, 6, 6, 6) dtr, then work {3 (3, 3)}; 4 (4, 4, 5, 5) trtr, fasten off, leaving rem sts unworked—{9 (10, 12)}; 14 (15, 17, 19, 19) sts; skip next {18 (20, 20)}; 22 (24, 26, 28, 30) sts, join MC in next st to work other shoulder, 5ch (counts as trtr), work {2 (2, 2)}; 3 (3, 3, 4, 4) trtr, then work {3 (3, 4)}; 5 (5, 6, 6, 6) dtr, then work {3 (4, 5)}; 5 (6, 7, 8, 8) tr to shoulder edge, fasten off—{9 (10, 12)}; 14 (15, 17, 19, 19) sts.

FRONT
Work same as Back until armhole measures approx {5.1 cm}; 5.1 (7.6, 10.2, 12.7, 12.7) cm, ending with a WS row.

LEFT FRONT
Next Row (RS): Work in next row of pattern across first 18 (20, 22)}; 25 (27, 30, 33, 34) sts.

Work even in pattern on 18 (20, 22)}; 25 (27, 30, 33, 34) sts until Left Front measures {5.1 (7.6, 10.2) cm}; 11.4 cm from beg of neck opening, ending with a WS row.

Shape Neck

Next Row (RS): Work in next row of pattern across first {10 (11, 13)}; 15 (16, 18, 20, 20) sts from end, turn, leaving rem sts unworked.

Next Row: Work in next row of pattern, dec 1 st at neck edge—{9 (10, 12)}; 14 (15, 17, 19, 19) sts rem.

Work even in pattern until armhole measures {12.7, (15.2, 17.8) cm}; 19.1 (21.6, 24.1, 26.7, 29.2) cm, ending with a WS row. Shape shoulder as for Back, fasten off.

RIGHT FRONT

With RS facing, join yarn at centre Front. Work same as Left Front, reversing shaping. Fasten off.

SLEEVE (make 2)

Sleeve Bottom: With MC, work {33 (37, 41)}; 43ch.

Foundation Row (WS): Dc in 2nd ch from hook, dc in each ch across, turn—{32 (36, 40)}; 42 dc.

*Work Rows 1–10 of Track Stitch Pattern I, then work Rows 1–4 of Track Stitch Pattern II; rep from * until piece measures {22.9 (25.4, 27.9) cm}; 30.5 (34.3, 39.4, 41.9, 47) cm from beg, fasten off.

Sleeve Top: Work {31 (35, 37)}; 41 (45, 51 55, 61) ch.

Foundation Row (WS): Dc in 2nd ch from hook, dc in each ch across, turn—{30 (34, 36)}; 40 (44, 50 54, 60) dc.

Work Rows 3–10 of Track Stitch Pattern I, then work Rows 1–4 of Track Stitch Pattern II, then work Rows 1–10 of Track Stitch Pattern I, ending when desired size is reached.

AT SAME TIME inc 1 st at each end of every other row {1 (1, 2)}; 5 (6, 7, 7, 7) times—{32 (36, 40)}; 50 (56, 64, 68, 74) sts. Work even in pattern until piece measures {15.2 (17.8, 20.3) cm}; 22.9 cm from beg, ending with a trtr row.

Shape Sleeve Cap

Sl st in first {3}; 4 (5, 6, 6, 6) sts, 1ch, dc in same st, dc each st across to within last {2}; 3 (4, 5, 5, 5) sts, turn, leaving rem sts unworked—{28 (32, 36)}; 44 (48, 54, 58, 64) sts. Dec 1 st each end of next 2 rows—{24 (28, 32)}; 40 (44, 50, 54, 60) sts. Work even in pattern until Sleeve Top measures {15.2 (17.8, 20.3) cm}; 22.9 cm from beg. Fasten off.

FINISHING

With RS tog, dc Front to Back across shoulders. Leaving {3.8 cm}; 7.6 cm slits open from bottom edge on each side, dc side seams. Arrange Sleeve Bottom with foundation ch on left side (sideways). Place bottom edge of Sleeve Top next to top edge of Sleeve Bottom. With RS tog, dc Sleeve Top to Sleeve Bottom. With WS facing, fold Sleeve in half lengthwise, dc sleeve seam up to Cap shaping. Set in Sleeves and dc Sleeve Cap into armhole, easing in fullness.

Neck Trim: With RS facing, join yarn at one shoulder seam on neck edge, 1ch, dc evenly around neck edge, sl st in first dc to join. Fasten off.

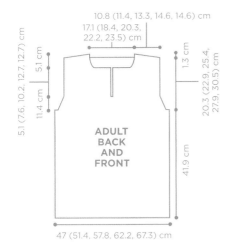

10.8 (11.4, 13.3, 14.6, 14.6) cm
17.1 (18.4, 20.3, 22.2, 23.5) cm
5.1 (7.6, 10.2, 12.7, 12.7) cm
5.1 cm
11.4 cm
1.3 cm
20.3 (22.9, 25.4, 27.9, 30.5) cm
41.9 cm

ADULT BACK AND FRONT

47 (51.4, 57.8, 62.2, 67.3) cm

38.7 (43.8, 50.2, 53.3, 57.8) cm
5.1 cm
17.8 cm

ADULT SLEEVE TOP

SLEEVE BOTTOM

33 cm

30.5 (34.3, 39.4, 41.9, 47) cm

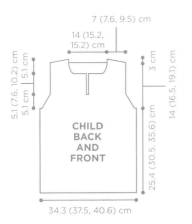

7 (7.6, 9.5) cm
14 (15.2, 15.2) cm
5.1 (7.6, 10.2) cm
5.1 cm
3 cm
14 (16.5, 19.1) cm
25.4 (30.5, 35.6) cm

CHILD BACK AND FRONT

34.3 (37.5, 40.6) cm

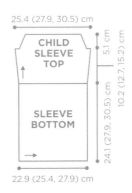

25.4 (27.9, 30.5) cm
5.1 cm
10.2 (12.7, 15.2) cm

CHILD SLEEVE TOP

SLEEVE BOTTOM

24.1 (27.9, 30.5) cm

22.9 (25.4, 27.9) cm

Net, Mesh, and Filet

NET, MESH, AND FILET

IN OUR CYBER-DRIVEN WORLD, THE NET IS A METAPHOR FOR, AND AN actuality of, our interconnectivity. But actual webs and nets are also some of our most utilitarian structures, basic to life. For centuries, they have been used to catch fish and other prey, to suspend weight in midair, and as transparent, breezy coverings to keep out insects. One would think early examples of crocheted netting would be plentiful, but none exists before the nineteenth century. Before then, nets were made (most often by men) with knotting and weaving techniques. Still, there is a major connection between the ancient art of net-making and the more recent development of crochet.

Lacis is an ancient form of net lace, also called nun's lace (it was made in convents, and lacis cushions graced cathedrals in the thirteenth century) or *filet brodé* (*filet* is French for *net*, and *brodé* for *embroidery*). Lacis consists of a delicate grid of net, knotted much like fishing net (the filet ground was sometimes produced by fishermen in the off season), upon which are embroidered elaborate pictures and florals. At the end of the eighteenth century, *tambouring* (an ancient chain-stitch embroidery technique, worked with a thin needlelike hook and known throughout Asia, the Middle East, and North Africa) was being done in France over less and less background fabric, until the background was eliminated entirely and it became "embroidery in air" and the crochet technique was born. Soon filet crochet was discovered as a less time-consuming method of producing pieces resembling lacis; with this method, the entire work—net and imagery—could be created at once. The coinciding birth of mass publishing fueled the development and popularity of crochet. Filet crochet was seen as a genteel woman's pastime, done with fancy crochet hooks carved in ivory with mother-of-pearl inlays, and many patterns were published for household trousseau items.

For this chapter, I've used four basic net stitches as allover patterns in projects as diverse as gloves, a capelet, a skirt, and a dress. I've also included a sweater in filet crochet. I like that the net patterns appear repetitive and gridlike while looking somewhat organic and handmade. These designs are at once wearable now and a trip into fashion history.

tiered capelet

This capelet features simple crocheted strips that are sandwiched between purchased ribbons of Cluny lace. The airy mesh of the ribbons resembles crochet, so it appears that you've executed a complex stitch with fine black thread.

Cluny lace is characterized by picot edges and geometric (often oval) lozenges on a gridlike ground. Originally handmade with multiple bobbins held on a pillow, this lace was so widely used by Victorians for trimming household items that the Leavers machine was invented to mass-produce it. Ironically, after the Industrial Revolution, thrifty crocheters began making edgings to imitate Cluny lace rather than purchasing the machine-made trim.

We can opt for manufactured over handmade and conventional over organic goods on a daily basis. These decisions are mostly based on economy of time and money, but when we have the luxury of considering the big picture, it's very satisfying to choose the handmade. It has become a balancing act of modern life.

>> See pattern on page 44.

fishnet funnelneck dress

This design combines two favorite fashions of the 1960s: the minidress and fishnet tights. Mod and clean, white lends it a minimalist look. It's a tribute to London designer Mary Quant, the self-proclaimed inventor of the miniskirt as well as other signature fashion items of the '60s, like hot pants and tall plastic boots. Mandy Hoeymakers has written a wonderful profile on Quant's amazing career at www.geocities.com/fashionavenue/catwalk/1038/quant.html, where you can also search for other innovators and trends of the decade.

>> See pattern on page 46.

bullion hem gloves

Unless you are doing a Michael Jackson number or an impersonation of Jackie O, gloves that are other than utilitarian appear rather conspicuous. Dress gloves are a rare sight. However, as recently as the 1960s, it was unacceptable for a woman to appear in public with ungloved hands, and there were still dizzying lists of the "do's and don'ts" of glove-wearing. You can check out the guidelines of glove etiquette from a 1961 handbook at a site called "Miss Abigail's Time Warp Advice: Classic Advice for Contemporary Dilemmas" at www.missabigail.com/advice/q103.html. These gloves are a nod to the ladylike gloves (often crocheted) that used to be mandatory, yet they are functionally warm in merino wool.

>> See pattern on page 49.

filet orchid boatneck

Filet has been a popular crochet technique since its inception in the early- to mid-nineteenth century, which coincided with the birth of mass publishing. Vintage patterns for filet crochet abound, featuring pictures and letters created by filling in or leaving blank the spaces of a regular grid. These early patterns were mostly for household items; done in very fine thread, they featured whole texts (psalms and such) in stylized script or idyllic pastoral pictures.

Most twentieth-century examples of filet are doilies, antimacassars, and bedspreads worked in starched white cotton. I discovered, upon examining many lovely vintage examples of filet roses and birds, that even this thread is still finer than today's sport or DK weight. In order to design my own filet sweater to be both quickly made and wearable, I chose a silk-blend yarn that is comparably softer than a cotton yarn of the same gauge. I opted for a stylized orchid filet motif I found in a stitch dictionary, attracted by its Art Nouveau quality.

>> See pattern on page 52.

picot mesh skirt

It's amazing how adding a tiny jutting dot (picot) to each diamond of crochet mesh takes an otherwise straightforward grid into rhythmic and spicy territory. *Picot* is from the Old French word *piquer*, meaning to prick or quilt. It has the same root as the modern verb *piquer*, meaning to provoke or arouse, and the noun *pique*, meaning a state of vexation. It is also related to *piquant*—spicy or stimulating. Who would have thought that so many pricking sensations—emotional, flavorful, tactile, and visual—would all be related? Myself an ardent fan of the burning taste and rush of endorphins delivered by chili peppers, I should have made this connection before searching the etymology of *picot*.

This sheer skirt can be worn with a slip or over leggings. I've added a pineapple-like edging to the hem, but beginners can leave it off if intimidated.

>> See pattern on page 56.

tiered capelet

OVERVIEW

You will work into the edges of lengths of purchased picot ribbon. You will insert hook in recessed inverted picot between the raised picots so the raised picots fall to RS of fabric. The crocheted fabric is gathered in at the ribbon due to the spacing of picots. Ribbon A has 15 recessed areas between picots to work into per 10.2 cm of ribbon. Ribbon B has 10 recessed areas between picots to work into per 10.2 cm of ribbon. The ribbon determines the width of pieces so if you use ribbon with different number of picots per centimetre than these then go by ribbon length, working approximately 15 dc per 10.2 cm section on Ribbon A and approx 10 dc per 10.2 cm section on Ribbon B.

FIRST TIER

Work foundation row over straight edge of Ribbon A, hooking in recessed inverted picot between the raised picots as follows:

Foundation Row (WS): With WS of Ribbon A facing, skip first 35.6 cm of ribbon for tie, join yarn in next space on straight edge of Ribbon A, 1ch, *dc in space, 1ch; rep from * 119 (133, 147,

Fitting Tip: Measure around shoulders and largest part of upper body including arms, and make closest size.

Shown in smallest size

MEASUREMENTS

Around shoulders 96.5 (106, 115.6, 125.1, 134.6) cm closed with 15.2 cm opening for ribbons

Around upper body 111.8 (122.6, 132.7, 143.5, 154.3) cm closed with 20.3 cm opening for ribbons

Length from top to hem 29.2 cm

YARN

Knit One, Crochet Too "Richesse et Soie" (65% cashmere /35% silk), fingering weight yarn. 3 (3, 4, 4, 5) balls

(.88 oz/25 g; 145 yd/132 m) in #9633 cornflower

HOOKS

2.25 mm (US 1) or size to needed to obtain gauge

NOTIONS

2 (2, 2, 2 1/2, 2 1/2) metre picot-edged Cluny lace cotton ribbon 3.8 cm wide with 1 scalloped edge and 1 straight edge (with approx

15 spaces per 10.2 cm section of lace) (Ribbon A)

4 (4, 4 1/2, 4 1/2, 5) metre picot-edged Cluny lace cotton ribbon 5.1 cm wide with 2 straight edges (with approx 10 spaces per 10.2 cm section of lace across each side) (Ribbon B)

Sewing needle and thread to match ribbon

GAUGE

28 sts and 14 rows = 10.2 cm in Easy Mesh Stitch Pattern. *(Note: For this project the stitch pattern gauge is not as important to sizing as the spacing of picots on the ribbons.)*

Always check and MATCH gauge for best results.

161, 175) times (or 20.3 cm less than desired length to fit around shoulders), dc in next space, turn.

Row 1 (RS): 4ch, *2 tr into next 1ch space, 1ch, rep from *, ending with 2 tr in last 1ch space, turn.

Row 2: 4ch, *2 tr into next 1ch space, 1ch, rep from *, ending with 2 tr in t-ch, turn.

Rows 3–11: Rep Row 2.

Joining First Ribbon B: Joining Row (WS): With WS of Ribbon B facing, skip first 35.6 cm of ribbon for tie, insert hook in next space on Ribbon B, draw yarn through, yo, draw yarn through 2 loops on hook (dc made), *skip next tr on Row 11 of First Tier, sl st in next tr, insert hook into 1ch space and into next space on ribbon, draw yarn through, yo, draw yarn through 2 loops on hook (dc made); rep from * across, thus joining Ribbon B across Row 11, ending with dc into t-ch and ribbon, fasten off. Leaving at least 35.6 cm for tie, trim rem length of Ribbon B and A.

special stitches

EASY MESH STITCH PATTERN (multiple of 3 sts in Row 2)
Foundation Row (WS): With WS of Ribbon A facing, skip first 35.6 cm of ribbon for tie, join yarn in next space on straight edge of Ribbon A, 1ch, *dc in space, 1ch; rep from * for required length, dc in next space, turn.

Row 1 (RS): 4ch, *2 tr into next 1ch space, 1ch, rep from *, ending with 2 tr in last 1ch space, turn.

Row 2: 4ch, *2 tr into next 1ch space, 1ch, rep from * across, ending with 2 tr in t-ch, turn.

Rep Row 2 for pattern.

SECOND TIER
With WS facing, take up piece and work across free edge of joined Ribbon B, beg opposite where fastened off on last tier. Work Foundation Row and Rows 1–11 as for First Tier.

Joining Second Ribbon B: Leaving at least 35.6 cm of ribbon for tie, rep Joining Row to join Second Tier to Second Ribbon B. Leaving at least 35.6 cm for tie, trim rem length of Ribbon B.

FINISHING
Tie pairs of ribbon ends tog in bows at front and trim ends to desired length. With needle and thread finish off ends by rolling frayed edge slightly to WS and whip stitching over to make French hem.

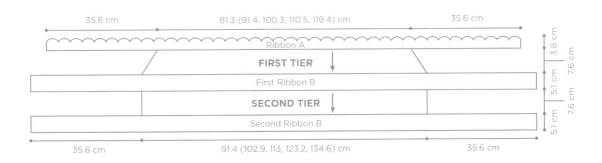

fishnet funnelneck dress

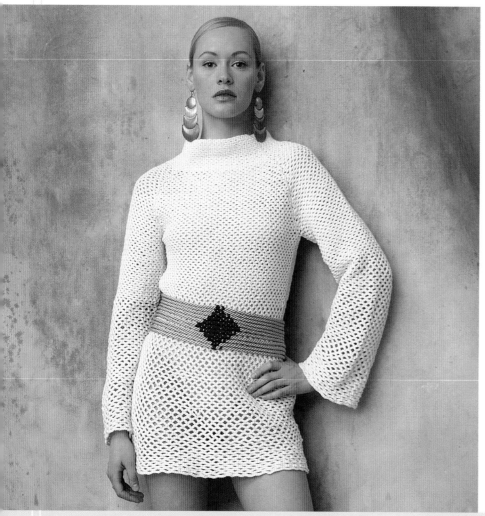

OVERVIEW

Sweater is made of four pieces (front and back and 2 sleeves) worked from hem up. The net pattern gets smaller towards top. Increases are made when changing to smaller net pattern to compensate for narrowing. Pieces are joined by crocheting together in netlike pattern.

BACK/FRONT (make 2)

Work 133 (143, 153, 163, 173, 183) ch. Beg 5ch Net Pattern as foll:

Foundation Row: 6ch for t-ch, dc in 9th ch from hook, *5ch, skip next 4 ch, dc in next ch; rep from * across, ending with dc in last ch, turn—27 (29, 31, 33, 35, 37) loops made.

Row 1: 6ch for t-ch, (dc, 5ch) in each 5ch loop across, ending with dc in t-ch, turn—27 (29, 31, 33, 35, 37) loops made.

Work even in 5ch Net Pattern as est until piece measures 33 cm from beg (*Note: If you would like a longer dress, work added length in pattern here*).

Beg 4ch Net Pattern, increasing 1 loop on each side on the initial row as foll:

Next Row: 5ch for t-ch, (dc, 4ch, dc, 4ch) in first loop, (dc, 4ch) in each loop across to t-ch, (dc, 4ch, dc) in

To fit with about 5.1 cm ease at chest

Shown in second size

MEASUREMENTS

Chest 86.4 (91.4, 96.5, 104.1, 109.2, 114.3) cm (pieces measure 41.9 [44.5, 47, 50.8, 53.3, 55.9] cm each, plus seaming adds 2.5 cm total)

Hem 111.8 (119.4, 129.5, 137.2, 144.8, 152.4) cm (pieces measure 54.6 [58.4, 63.5, 67.3, 71.1, 74.9] cm each, plus seaming adds 2.5 cm total)

Length 91.4 (94, 96.5, 96.5, 99.1, 101.6) cm

YARN

Lana Grossa "Point" (96% cotton/4% elastan) worsted weight yarn 12 (13, 15, 17, 19, 21) balls (1.75 oz/50 g; 120 yd/ 110 m) in #22 cream, (*Note: This yarn contains stretch fiber, which allows for fitting over head without neck opening; substitution of 100% cotton not recommended.*)

HOOKS

3.25 mm (US D/3) or size to match gauge

GAUGE

5 x 5ch loops and 11 rows = 10.2 cm in 5ch Net Pattern (gently stretched lengthwise);

6 4ch loops and 13 rows = 10.2 cm in 4ch Net Pattern

(gently stretched length-wise);

7 1/2 3ch loops and 16 rows = 10.2 cm in 3ch Net Pattern;

9 1/2 2ch loops and 20 rows = 10.2 cm in 2ch Net Pattern;

Always check and MATCH gauge for best results.

t-ch, turn—29 (31, 33, 35, 37, 39) loops made.

Work even in 4ch Net Pattern as est until piece measures 53.3 cm from beg (20.3 cm in this st pattern).

Beg 3ch Net Pattern, increasing 1 loop on each side on the initial row as foll:

Next Row: 4ch for t-ch, (dc, 3ch, dc, 3ch) in first loop, (dc, 3ch) in each loop across to t-ch, (3ch, dc, 3ch, dc) in t-ch, turn—31 (33, 35, 37, 39, 41) loops made.

Work even in 3ch Net Pattern as est until piece measures 66 cm from beg (12.7 cm in this st pattern).

Shape Raglan: Cont in 3ch Net Pattern, decrease at each side at a rate of 2 loops dec over 4 rows as foll:

Row 1 RS: Do not make t-ch, (dc, 3ch) in first loop, (dc, 3ch) in each loop across to t-ch, end dc in t-ch, turn—30 (32, 34, 36, 38, 40) loops made, turn.

Row 2: Do not make t-ch, (dc, 3ch) in first loop, (dc, 3ch) in each loop across to last loop, ending with dc in last loop, turn —29 (31, 33, 35, 37, 39) loops made.

Row 3: 4ch for t-ch, (dc, 3ch) in each loop across, ending with dc in last loop, turn—29 (31, 33, 35, 37, 39) loops made.

Row 4: 4ch for t-ch, (dc, 3ch) in each loop across, ending with dc in t-ch, turn—29 (31, 33, 35, 37, 39) loops made.

Rep last 4 rows 6 (7, 8, 8, 9, 10) times more [14 (16, 18, 18, 20, 22) loops decreased over 28 (32, 36, 36, 40, 44) rows]—17 (17, 17, 19, 19, 19) loops rem at end of last row.

5CH NET PATTERN
Ch a multiple of 5, plus 3.

Foundation Row: 6ch for t-ch, dc in 9th ch from hook, *5ch, skip next 4 ch, dc in next ch; rep from * across, ending with dc in last ch, turn.

Next and all rows: 6ch for t-ch, (dc, 5ch) in each 5ch loop across, ending with dc in t-ch, turn.

4CH NET PATTERN
All rows: 5ch for t-ch, (dc, 4ch) in each loop across, ending with dc in t-ch, turn.

3CH NET PATTERN
All rows: 4ch for t-ch, (dc, 3ch) in each loop across, ending with dc in t-ch, turn.

2CH NET PATTERN
All rows: 3ch for t-ch, (dc, 2ch) in each space across, ending with dc in t-ch, turn.

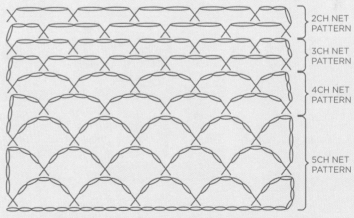

2CH NET PATTERN

3CH NET PATTERN

4CH NET PATTERN

5CH NET PATTERN

REDUCED SAMPLE OF NET PATTERNS

STITCH KEY

⬭ = chain (ch)

✕ = double crochet (dc)

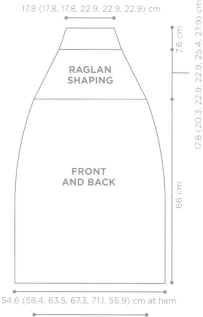

17.8 (17.8, 17.8, 22.9, 22.9, 22.9) cm

7.6 cm

RAGLAN SHAPING

17.8 (20.3, 22.9, 22.9, 25.4, 27.9) cm

FRONT AND BACK

66 cm

54.6 (58.4, 63.5, 67.3, 71.1, 55.9) cm at hem

41.9 (44.5, 47, 50.8, 53.3, 55.9) cm at bust

10.2 (10.2, 10.2, 12.7, 12.7, 12.7) cm

7.6 cm

RAGLAN SHAPING

17.8 (20.3, 22.9, 22.9, 25.4, 27.9) cm

SLEEVE

50.8 cm

33 (36.8, 40.6, 44.5, 48.3, 53.3) cm

Note: Piece should measure 17.8 (20.3, 22.9, 22.9, 25.4, 27.9) cm from beg of Raglan Shaping.

COLLAR

Work even in 2ch Net Pattern (without inc on initial row) until piece measures 91.4 (94, 96.5, 99.1, 101.6) cm from beg (7.6 cm in this st pattern). Fasten off.

SLEEVE (make 2)

Beg 5ch Net Pattern as foll:

Work 78 (88, 98, 108, 118, 128) ch.

Foundation Row: 6ch for t-ch, dc in 9th ch from hook, *5ch, skip next 4 ch, dc in next ch; rep from * across, ending with dc in last ch—16 (18, 20, 22, 24, 26) loops made.

Work even in 5ch Net pattern as est until piece measures 17.8 cm from beg.

Beg 4ch Net Pattern, increasing 2 loops on each side on the initial row as foll:

Next Row: 5ch for t-ch, (dc, 4ch, dc, 4ch) in each of first 2 loops, (dc, 4ch) in each loop across to last 2 loops, (dc, 4ch, dc, 4ch) in next loop, (dc, 4ch, dc) in t-ch—20 (22, 24, 26, 28, 30) loops made.

Work even in 4ch Net Pattern as est until piece measures 38.1 cm from beg (20.3 cm in this st pattern).

Beg 3ch Net Pattern, increasing 2 loops on each side on the initial row as foll:

Next Row: 4ch for t-ch, (dc, 3ch, dc, 3ch) in each of first 2 loops, (dc, 3ch) in each loop across to last 2 loops, (dc, 3ch, dc, 3ch) in next loop, (dc, 3ch, dc) in t-ch—24 (26, 28, 30, 32, 34) loops made.

Work even in 3ch Net Pattern as est until piece measures 50.8 cm from beg (12.7 cm in this st pattern).

Shape Raglan: Cont in 3ch Net Pattern as est, working the 4 row decrease as for Back/Front 7 (8, 9, 9, 10, 11) times total [14 (16, 18, 18, 20, 22) loops decreased over 28 (32, 36, 36, 40, 44) rows] —10 (10, 10, 12, 12, 12) loops rem at end of last row.

Note: Piece should measure 17.8 (20.3, 22.9, 22.9, 25.4, 27.9) cm from beg of Raglan Shaping.

COLLAR

Work even in 2ch Net Pattern (without inc on initial row) until piece

measures 91.4 (94, 96.5, 99.1, 101.6) cm from beg (7.6 cm in this st pattern).

FINISHING

Join each Sleeve to Raglan and Collar at Front and Back; join Front and Back pieces at side seams; join Sleeves from cuff to beg Raglan shaping as follows:

Raglan Joining Row: Hold Front and one Sleeve piece with RS together and WS facing outward, join raglan seam beg at neck as follows: Sl st in edge st of both pieces at once to join, (1ch, sl st in next set of 2ch spaces of both pieces) across Collar to base of neck with RS facing, *1ch, sl st in next ch loop on Sleeve, 1ch, sl st in next ch loop on Body; rep from * across to underarm. Fasten off. Rep Sleeve Joining Row on Back of same Sleeve. Rep Raglan Joining Row on Front and Back to join other Sleeve.

Side Joining Row: With RS of Front and Back facing, join yarn with sl st in first 5ch loop at bottom edge of Front, *2ch, sl st in next ch loop on Back, 2ch, sl st in next ch loop on Front; rep from * across 5ch and 4ch Net Pattern, **1ch, sl st in next ch loop on Back, 1ch, sl st in next ch loop on Front; rep from ** across 3ch Net Pattern to underarm. Fasten off. Rep Side Joining Row on other side of dress.

Sleeve Joining Row: Fold Sleeve in half lengthwise, with WS tog, join yarn with sl st in first 5ch space on one side edge cuff, * 2ch, sl st in next ch loop on opposite side edge, 2ch, sl st in next ch loop on first edge; rep from * across 5ch and 4ch Net Pattern, **1ch, sl st in next ch loop on opposite edge, 1ch, sl st in next ch loop on first edge; rep from ** across 3ch Net Pattern to underarm. Fasten off. Rep Sleeve Joining Row to join other Sleeve seam.

NECK EDGING

With RS facing, join yarn in any 2ch space at back neck, 1ch, (dc, 2ch) in each space around neck opening, sl st in first dc to join.

bullion hem gloves

To fit woman's size medium (try on your own hand as you work to customize fit)

MEASUREMENTS
19.1 cm in circumference around palm unstretched

YARN
Louet Sales "Gems Pearl" (100% merino, washable), fingering weight yarn

2 hanks (1.75 oz/50 g/ 172 yd/66 m) in #80 aqua

HOOK
2.25 mm (US steel 2)

NOTIONS
Stitch markers or smooth contrasting yarn for markers
Tapestry/darning needle

GAUGE
8 sts and 8 rows = 2.5 cm in (dc, 1ch) mesh stitch pattern measured unstretched.
Always check and MATCH gauge for best results.

OVERVIEW

Glove is worked from fingertips to wrist. Each finger is worked separately in spiral rounds, then joined and hand worked in spiral rounds; thumb is joined and decreases made at base of thumb to wrist; cuff is worked in rows, leaving a slit on outside of glove.

left glove
INDEX FINGER

3ch, join with sl st in first ch to form ring.

Rnd 1: 2ch (counts as dc, 1ch), (dc, 1ch) in ring 5 times, do not join—12 sts; 6 1ch spaces made. Work in a spiral, marking beg of each rnd and moving marker up as work progresses.

Rnd 2 (inc rnd): (Dc, 1ch, dc, 1ch) in next 2ch space, (dc, 1ch) in each ch space around—14 sts; 7 1ch spaces made.

Rnds 3-4: Rep Rnd 2—18 sts, 9 1ch spaces at end of last rnd.

Try this fingertip "cap" on intended wearer's index finger. If necessary add or eliminate an increase rnd.

Next Rnd (even): (Dc, 1ch) in each ch space around—18 sts; 9 1ch spaces.

Cont to work even until Index Finger measures 6.4 cm from beg or desired length to fit to base of index finger, sl st in next dc to join. Fasten off.

SECOND FINGER

Work same as Index Finger, working even until Second Finger measures 7 cm from beg or desired length to fit to base of second finger. Fasten off.

special stitches

BULLION STITCH

Wrap yarn 14 times around shaft of hook, insert hook in st and pull up a loop, yo and draw through every loop on hook *(Tip: I use left thumb and index finger to pinch the tight wraps and drop them off the hook one by one while pulling the hook through).*

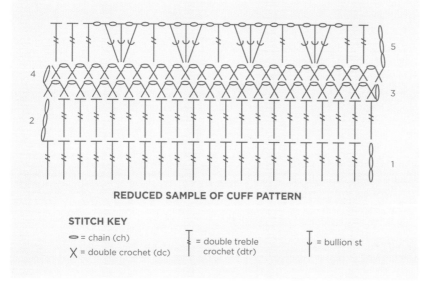

REDUCED SAMPLE OF CUFF PATTERN

STITCH KEY

⬭ = chain (ch)

X = double crochet (dc)

⌶ = double treble crochet (dtr)

↓ = bullion st

RING FINGER

Work same as Index Finger, working even until Ring Finger measures 6.4 cm from beg or desired length to fit to base of ring finger. Fasten off.

PINKY

3ch, join with sl st in first ch to form ring.

Rnd 1: 2ch (counts as dc, 1ch), (dc, 1ch) in ring 5 times—12 sts; 6 1ch spaces made. Work in a spiral as before.

Rnd 2 (inc rnd): (Dc, 1ch, dc, 1ch) in next 2ch space, (dc, 1ch) in each ch space around—14 sts; 7 1ch spaces made.

Try this fingertip "cap" on intended wearer's pinky. If necessary, add or eliminate an increase rnd.

Cont to work even until Pinky measures 5.7 cm from beg or desired length to fit to base of pinky. Fasten off.

THUMB

3ch, join with sl st in first ch to form ring.

Rnd 1: 2ch (counts as dc, 1ch), (dc, 1ch) in ring 5 times—12 sts; 6 1ch spaces made. Work in a spiral as before.

Rnd 2 (inc rnd): (Dc, 1ch, dc, 1ch) in next 2ch space, (dc, 1ch) in each ch space around—14 sts; 7 1ch spaces made.

Rnds 3-7: Rep Rnd 2—24 sts, 12 1ch spaces at end of last rnd.

Try this fingertip "cap" on intended wearer's thumb. If necessary, add or eliminate one of the increase rnds.

Cont to work even until Thumb measures 6.4 cm from beg or desired length to fit to base of thumb, sl st in next dc to join. Fasten off.

Joining Fingers: Lay fingers out with fingertips facing down aligned from right to left in order: Pinky, Ring

Finger, Second Finger, Index Finger. Beg of rnd will be outer pinky edge and you'll work across back of hand first. You will pick up 68 sts as foll: *(Note: If you have adjusted the number of increases you'll need to leave extra sts unworked between fingers to darn later or, in the case of increases not made, work twice in some finger sts to get proper number of sts for palm width.)*

HAND

Rnd 1: With RS of each finger facing, join yarn with slip st in any 1ch space on last rnd of Pinkie, 1ch, dc in first 1ch space, 1ch, (dc, 1ch) in each of next 3 1ch spaces—8 sts; 4 1ch spaces made *(Note: Leave rem 3 1ch spaces of Pinky unworked.)*; take up Ring Finger, dc in any 1ch space in last rnd of Ring Finger, 1ch, (dc, 1ch) in each of next 3 1ch spaces—8 sts; 4 1ch spaces *(Note: Leave rem 5 1ch spaces of Ring Finger unworked)*; take up Second Finger, dc in any 1ch space in last rnd of Second Finger, 1ch, (dc, 1ch) in each of next 3 1ch spaces—8 sts; 4 1ch spaces *(Note: Leave rem 5 1ch spaces of Second Finger unworked)*; take up Index Finger, dc in any 1ch space in last rnd of Index Finger, 1ch, (dc, 1ch) in each 1ch space around—18 sts; 9 1ch spaces; working across palm side of fingers; (dc, 1ch) in each rem 1ch space across Second Finger—10 sts; 5 1ch spaces; (dc, 1ch) in each rem 1ch space across Ring Finger—10 sts; 5 1ch spaces; (dc, 1ch) in each rem 1ch space across Pinky—6 sts; 3 1ch spaces, do not join—68 sts; 34 1ch spaces. Cont to work in a spiral as before.

Cont to work even until Hand measures 5.1 cm from beg or desired length to fit to base of thumb.

Joining Thumb: *(Note: Working in a spiral may have caused stitches to shift. Place a marker in centre dc on outside edge of Index Finger side of Hand.)*

Next Rnd (join inner edge of Thumb): (Dc, 1ch) in each 1ch space across to marker, take up Thumb piece, with

WS of Thumb facing, dc in any 1ch space in last rnd of Thumb, 1ch, (dc, 1ch) in each of next 5 1ch spaces of Thumb (Note: Leave rem 6 1ch spaces of Thumb unworked), skip next 6 1ch spaces on Hand, dc in next 1ch space on Hand, 1ch, (dc, 1ch) in each 1ch space across palm—68 sts; 34 1ch spaces.

Next Rnd (join outer edge of Thumb): (Dc, 1ch) in each 1ch space across back of Hand to Thumb, working across rem side of Thumb, with RS of Thumb facing, (dc, 1ch) in each of next 6 1ch spaces, skip 12 sts (6 1ch spaces) on outer edge of Thumb, working across back of Hand, (dc, 1ch) in each 1ch space across—68 sts; 34 1ch spaces.

Shape Thumb Gusset: Place a marker in first and last 1ch space at base of Thumb, move markers up as work progresses. Dec 2 sts (one 1ch space) on each side of thumb gusset every row 5 times as foll:

Next Rnd (dec rnd): (Dc, 1ch) in each 1ch space across to first marker, skip next 1ch space, slm, (dc, 1ch) in each 1ch space to next marker, skip next 1ch space, slm, (dc, 1ch) in each rem 1ch space around—64 sts; 32 1ch spaces.

Rep last rnd (4 times)—48 sts; 24 1ch spaces at end of last rnd.

Work even in est patt for 8 rnds.

Next Rnd: Dc in each dc and each 1ch space around, sl st in first dc to join—48 dc made.

Next Rnd: 3ch (counts as dtr), skip first dc, dtr in each dc around, sl st in top of t-ch, turn—48 sts.

CUFF
Work now progresses in rows.

Row 1 (RS): 3ch (counts as dtr), skip first st, dtr in each st across, do not join, turn—48 sts.

Row 2: 3ch (counts as dtr), skip first st, dtr in each st across, turn—48 sts.

Row 3: 1ch, dc in first dtr, 1ch, (dc, 1ch) in each dtr across, ending with dc in top of t-ch, turn—97 sts; 48 1ch spaces.

Row 4: 1ch, skip first dc, (dc, 1ch) in each 1ch space across, ending with dc in top of t-ch, turn—96 sts; 48 1ch spaces.

Row 5 (bullion row): 3ch (counts as dtr), (skip next 1ch space, dtr in next dc) twice, *1ch, skip next 2 1ch spaces, (bullion st, 1ch) 3 times in next dc, skip next 2 1ch spaces, dtr in next dc; rep from * 10 times, (skip next 1ch space, dtr in next dc) twice—11 bullion shells. Do not fasten off.

Slit Trim: Dc evenly down left edge of Cuff slit, dc evenly up right edge of Cuff slit. Fasten off.

Darn sts together between fingers. Fasten off.

right hand
Work same as Left Hand until Joining of Fingers. Arrange fingers as for Left Hand. (Note: For Right Hand, you will beg by working across palm, then proceed to work across back of hand.)

HAND
Rnd 1: With RS of each finger facing, join yarn with slip st in any 1ch space on last rnd of Pinkie, 1ch, dc in first 1ch space, 1ch, (dc, 1ch) in each of next 3 1ch spaces—8 sts; 4 1ch spaces made (Note: Leave rem 3 1ch spaces of Pinkie unworked.); take up Ring Finger, dc in any 1ch space in last rnd of Ring Finger, 1ch, (dc, 1ch) in each of next 4 1ch spaces—10 sts; 5 1ch spaces (Note: Leave rem 4 1ch spaces of Ring Finger unworked.); take up Second Finger, dc in any 1ch space in last rnd of Second Finger, 1ch, (dc, 1ch) in each of next 4 1ch spaces—10 sts; 5 1ch spaces (Note: Leave rem 4 1ch spaces of Second Finger unworked); take up Index Finger, dc in any 1ch space in last rnd of Index Finger, 1ch, (dc, 1ch) in each 1ch space around—18 sts;

9 1ch spaces; working across palm side of fingers; (dc, 1ch) in each rem 1ch space across Second Finger—8 sts; 4 1ch spaces; (dc, 1ch) in each rem 1ch space across Ring Finger—8 sts; 4 1ch spaces; (dc, 1ch) in each rem 1ch space across Pinky—6 sts; 3 1ch spaces, do not join—68 sts; 34 1ch spaces. Cont to work in a spiral as before.

Cont to work even until Hand measures 5.1 cm from beg or desired length to fit to base of thumb.

Joining Thumb: (Note: Place a marker in centre dc on outside edge of Index Finger side of Hand.)

Next Rnd (join inner edge of Thumb): (Dc, 1ch) in each 1ch space across to within 6 1ch spaces of marker, take up Thumb piece, with WS of Thumb facing, dc in any 1ch space in last rnd of Thumb, 1ch, (dc, 1ch) in each of next 5 1ch spaces of Thumb (Note: Leave rem 6 1ch spaces of Thumb unworked), skip next 6 1ch spaces on Hand, dc in next 1ch space, 1ch, (dc, 1ch) in each 1ch space across back of Hand—68 sts; 34 1ch spaces.

Next Rnd (join outer edge of Thumb): (Dc, 1ch) in each 1ch space across palm of Hand to Thumb, working across rem side of Thumb, with RS of Thumb facing, (dc, 1ch) in each of next 6 1ch spaces, working across palm of Hand, (dc, 1ch) in each 1ch space across—68 sts; 34 1ch spaces.

Finish same as Left Hand (Cuff Slit will be at Pinky side edge).

filet orchid boatneck

MEASUREMENTS
Bust 92.7 (101.6, 110.5) cm
Length 50.8 (53.3, 54.6) cm
Shown in smallest size

YARN
Jaeger "Trinity" (40%
silk/35% cotton/25% poly-
amide), dk weight yarn

6 (8, 10) balls (1.75 oz/
50 g; 218 yd/200 m) in
#449 water

HOOKS
2.75 mm (US steel 1) or size
to match gauge
2.25 mm (US steel 2) for
finishing

NOTIONS
Six 6 mm satin-covered
metal post buttons

GAUGE
9 spaces or blocks and
12 rows = 10.2 cm in filet
crochet over charted stitch
pattern.

Always check and MATCH
gauge for best results.

OVERVIEW
This pullover is worked in one piece
from back hem up to neck then over
the shoulders and down the front.
*(Note: Stated gauge is an average.
Filled blocks are slightly larger than
spaces.)* If you forget to fill in a block
you can work 2 tr over the block after
piece is done; however you cannot
undo a filled in block without undo-
ing the piece back to the error. So
be sure to check every few rows that
work matches chart.

SWEATER
Sweater is worked in blocks and
spaces following a chart. Read all
odd-numbered rows from right to left
and all even-numbered rows from left
to right.

BACK
Starting at bottom edge, with larger
hook, work 87 (99, 111) ch plus 3 (first
tr t-ch) plus 2 (first space).

Row 1: Tr in 8th ch from hook (first
space made), (2ch, skip next 2 ch,
tr in next ch) 7 (9, 11) times (7 [9, 11]
spaces made), tr in each of next 18
ch (6 blocks made), 2ch, skip next 2
ch, tr in next ch (centre space made),
tr in each of next 18 ch (6 blocks
made), (2ch, skip next 2 ch, tr in next
ch) 8 (10, 12) times (8 [10, 12] spaces
made), turn—29 (33, 37) blocks and
spaces made (first row of chart complete).

Rows 2–56 (2–58, 2–60): Work in
blocks and spaces following chart.
Following chart, inc 1 block or space
at beg of Rows 13 and 14; 19 and 20;
23 and 24; 27 and 28; 31 and 32; 33
and 34; then inc 4 spaces at the beg
of Rows 35 and 36; inc 6 spaces and
blocks at beg of Rows 37–46. Then
work even on 109 (113, 117) blocks and
spaces to shoulder shaping.

BACK RIGHT SHOULDER
Row 57 (59, 61): Work following chart
across first 48 (50, 52) blocks and
spaces to neck edge, turn.

Rows 58-60 (60-62, 62-64): Work in blocks and spaces following chart for right shoulder only, decreasing 1 space at neck edge of each row.

Rotate chart 180 degrees to beg Front Right Shoulder.

FRONT RIGHT SHOULDER

Rows 61-64 (63-66, 65-68): Work in blocks and spaces following chart beginning with last row of chart for desired size. Work first 4 rows of chart, increasing 1 space at neck edge on each of last 3 rows. Fasten off.

Rotate chart 180 degrees to work Back Left Shoulder.

BACK LEFT SHOULDER

Row 57 (59, 61): With RS of Back facing, skip first 13 blocks and spaces to the left of last st made in first row of Back Right Shoulder, using larger hook, join yarn in next tr, 3ch, work in blocks and spaces across left side of Back following chart for left shoulder.

Rows 58-60 (60-62, 62-64): Work in blocks and spaces following chart for left shoulder only, decreasing 1 space at neck edge of each row.

Rotate chart 180 degrees to beg Front Left Shoulder.

FRONT LEFT SHOULDER

Rows 61-64 (63-66, 65-68): Work in blocks and spaces following chart beginning with last row of chart for desired size. Work first 4 rows of chart, increasing 1 space at neck edge on each of last 3 rows. Drop loop from hook to be picked up later.

With WS facing, using larger hook, join a separate strand of yarn in last tr of last row of Front Right Shoulder, 38ch for front neck, sl st in top of first st of last row of Front Left Shoulder. Fasten off strand.

FRONT

Row 65 (67, 69): Pick up dropped loop at end of Row 64 (66, 68) of Front Left Shoulder, following chart, work in blocks and spaces across Front Left Shoulder, cont to work across ch at neck opening, cont to work across Front Right Shoulder, turn—109 (113, 117) blocks and spaces.

Rows 66-120 (68-124, 70-128): Work in blocks and spaces following upside down chart. *(Note: All decreasing will occur at the ends of rows.)*

SWEATER EDGING

With RS of sweater facing, using smaller hook, join yarn in bottom left-hand corner of back bottom edge, 3ch, tr evenly around entire sweater edge, working tr in each st across bottom edge, 3 tr in corner st, tr evenly across side edge, *(Note: Work [tr, dc, tr] in inc corners to even out shaping if desired)*, 3 tr at corner of cuff edges, cont to work around entire sweater edge in same manner, sl st in 3rd ch of t-ch to join. Fasten off.

FINISHING

Right Side Seam: With RS of Front and Back together, matching sts across sides and underarm, with smaller hook, working through double thickness of front and back, join yarn at cuff end of sleeve, 1ch, dc evenly across underarm and down side edge to within 10.2 cm of bottom edge. Fasten off, leaving 10.2 cm open for slit.

Left Side Seam: Work same as Right Side Seam, joining to within 203 cm of bottom edge. Fasten off.

Button Loop Row: With RS of Front facing, mark positions for 6 button loops across front left slit edge, placing 1 marker 10.2 cm above bottom edge, 1 marker 1.3 cm below top of slit and 4 markers evenly spaced between. With RS facing, using smaller hook, join yarn approximately 8.9 cm above bottom edge on front left slit edge, sl st evenly across slit edge, working (sl st, 6ch, sl st) at each marker. Fasten off. Sew 1 button to back left slit edge opposite each button loop.

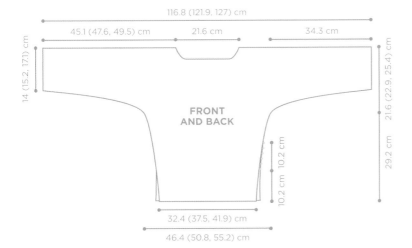

FRONT AND BACK

116.8 (121.9, 127) cm

45.1 (47.6, 49.5) cm   21.6 cm   34.3 cm

14 (15.2, 17.1) cm

21.6 (22.9, 25.4) cm

29.2 cm

10.2 cm 10.2 cm

32.4 (37.5, 41.9) cm

46.4 (50.8, 55.2) cm

special stitches

FILET CROCHET

Work in blocks and spaces (defined below) following the chart. 3ch at beg of each row (counts as first tr).

Space (symbolized by empty box): 2ch, skip next 2 sts, tr in next tr.

Block (symbolized by dot in box) over space: 2 tr in next 2ch space, tr in next tr.

Block (symbolized by dot in box) over block: Tr in each of next 3 tr.

To decrease one or more spaces at beg of row: Sl st to designated tr, 3ch (for first tr) to beg row.

To decrease one or more spaces at end of row: Work to designated tr, then turn to beg next row, 3ch (for first tr).

To increase one or more spaces at beg or end of row: See illustrations and text.

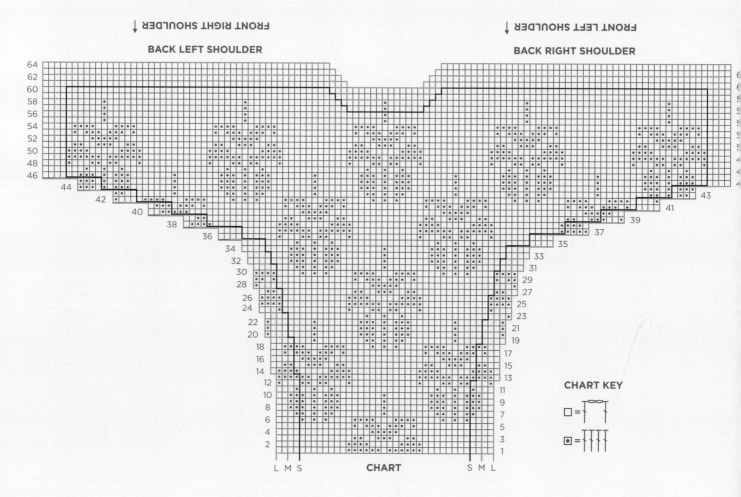

INCREASING IN FILET CROCHET

Increasing 1 Space at Beg of Row: At end of previous row, 2ch (bottom of space), + 3ch (first tr), + 2ch (first space), turn, tr in last tr of previous row (1 space inc made), cont across following chart.

Increasing More Than 1 Space at Beg of Row: At end of previous row, 2ch (for first additional space), 3ch more for each additional space, + 3ch (first tr), + 2ch (first space), turn, tr in 8th ch from hook (first space inc made), *2ch, skip next 2 ch, tr in next st; rep from * across added ch, ending with tr in first tr of previous row, cont across following chart.

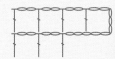

Increasing 1 Block at Beg of Row: At end of previous row, 2ch (bottom of block), + 3ch (first tr), turn, tr in 4th ch from hook, tr in next ch (1 block inc made), tr in last tr of previous row, cont across following chart.

Increasing More Than 1 Block at Beg of Row: At end of previous row, 2ch (for first additional block), 3ch more for each additional block, + 3ch (first tr), tr in 4th ch from hook, tr in next ch (first block inc made), *tr in each of next 3 sts; rep from * across added ch for each added block, ending with tr in first tr of previous row, cont across following chart.

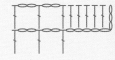

Increasing 1 Space at End of Row: Work following chart to end of row, 2ch (for inc space), yo (4 times), insert hook in same place as last tr made, yo, draw through st, (yo, draw through 2 loops on hook) 5 times to complete quad tr (1 space inc made).

STITCH KEY

⬭ = chain (ch)

┬ = treble crochet (tr)

= quad treble crochet (quad tr)

picot mesh skirt

OVERVIEW

Skirt is worked from waist down in rnds of Picot Mesh Pattern.

SKIRT

Work 180 (198, 216, 234, 252, 270) ch, and without twisting ch, join with sl st in first ch.

Rnd 1: *5ch, skip next 5ch, dc in next ch, picot; rep from * around, ending with dc in first ch at beg of foundation ch, picot, do not join. Work in a continuous spiral (beg of rnd will shift) as follows:

Next and all rnds: *5ch, dc in next 5ch loop, picot; rep from * around, do not join.

Continue to work in spiraling rnds of Picot Mesh Pattern until piece measures 45.7 cm from beg, ending last rep with 5ch, approx aligned with where foundation ch was joined.

DECORATIVE HEM

Rnd 1: Dc in next 5ch loop, place a marker in this dc to mark beg of rnd,

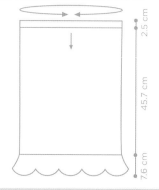

76.2 (83.8, 91.4, 99.1, 106.7, 114.3) cm

2.5 cm

45.7 cm

7.6 cm

Sizing Tip: This piece has no shaping and relies on elasticity of stitch and yarn; choose a size that will stretch to fit widest part of hips.

Shown in second smallest size

MEASUREMENTS

Low waist/high hip 76.2 (83.8, 91.4, 99.1, 106.7, 114.3) cm; stretches 7.6 cm to fit widest hip 83.8 (91.4, 99.1, 106.7, 114.3, 121.9) cm

Length 56 cm

YARN

Lana Grossa "Point" (96% cotton/4% elastan) worsted weight yarn

4 (5, 5, 6, 7, 7) balls (1.75 oz/50 g; 120 yd/110 m) in #18 black; this yarn contains stretch fiber, which allows for fitting over hips without waist opening or much shaping; substitution of 100% cotton not recommended.

HOOK

3.25 mm (D/3) or size needed to obtain gauge

GAUGE

24 sts (4 5ch loops) and 10 rnds = 10.2 cm in Picot Mesh Pattern.

Always check and MATCH gauge for best results.

For your gauge swatch, make a fingerless mitt (shown on boy next to girl in flower hat on page 114) as follows:

Work 42ch loosely, and without twisting ch, join with sl st in first ch. Work in rnds of Picot Mesh Pattern for 12.7 cm to check gauge.

*5ch, dc in next 5ch loop; rep from * around, ending with 5ch, sl st in first dc to join—30 (33, 36, 39, 42, 45) 5ch loops (Note: Must have a multiple of 3 loops to work pattern).

Rnd 2: 1ch, *6 dc in next 5ch loop, 5 dc in next 5ch loop, 6 dc in next 5ch loop; rep from * around, sl st in first dc to join—170 (187, 204, 221, 238, 255) dc.

Rnd 3: 7ch (counts as tr, 4ch), skip first 4 dc, *dc in each of next 9 dc [should be centered over 3 loops, 2 over first loop; 5 over 2nd loop; and 2 over 3rd loop], 4ch, skip next 4 dc**, (tr, 2ch, tr) bet next 2 dc [this should be exactly between 3rd and 4th loops], 4ch, skip next 4 dc; rep from * around, ending last rep at **, tr in same space as 7ch at beg of rnd, 2ch, sl st in 3rd ch of 7ch at beg of rnd to join.

Rnd 4: 8ch (counts as tr, 5ch), skip next 4ch loop and next dc, *dc in each of next 7 dc, 5ch, skip next dc and 4ch loop, tr in next tr, 2ch, (tr, 2ch, tr) in next 2ch space, 2ch**, tr in next tr, 5ch, skip next 4ch loop and next dc; rep from * ending last rep at **, sl st in 3rd ch of 8ch at beg of rnd to join.

Rnd 5: 8ch (counts as tr, 5ch), skip next 5ch loop and next dc, *dc in each of next 5 dc, 5ch, skip next dc and 5ch loop, (tr, 2ch) in each of next 2 tr, (tr, 2ch, tr) in next 2ch space**, (2ch, tr) in each of next 2 tr, 5ch, skip next 5ch loop and next dc; rep from

* around, ending last rep at **, 2ch, tr in next tr, 2ch, sl st in 3rd ch of 8ch at beg of rnd to join.

Rnd 6: 8ch (counts as tr, 5ch), skip next 5ch loop and next dc, *dc in each of next 3 dc, 5ch, skip next dc and 5ch loop, (tr, 2ch) in each of next 3 tr, (tr, 2ch, tr) in next 2ch space**, (2ch, tr) in each of next 3 tr, 5ch, skip next 5ch loop and next dc; rep from * around, ending last rep at **, (2ch, tr) in each of next 2 tr, 2ch, sl st in 3rd ch of 8ch at beg of rnd to join.

Rnd 7: 1ch, dc in first st, 5ch, skip next 5ch loop and next dc, *dc in next dc, 5ch, skip next dc and 5ch loop, [dc in next tr, (dc, picot) in next 2ch space] 7 times**, dc in next tr, 5ch, skip next 5ch loop and next dc; rep from * around, ending last rep at **, sl st first dc to join. Fasten off.

special stitches

PICOT
3ch, sl st in last dc made.

PICOT MESH PATTERN
Work a multiple of 6ch, join.

Rnd 1: *5ch, skip next 5ch, dc in next ch, picot; rep from * around, ending with dc in first ch at beg of foundation ch at base of first 5ch, picot, do not join. Work in a continuous spiral (beg of rnd will shift) as follows:

Next and all rnds: *5ch, dc in next 5ch loop, picot; rep from * around, do not join.

FINISHING

Waistband: Rnd 1: With RS facing, working across opposite side of foundation ch, join yarn at base of first dc in Foundation Row, 3ch (counts as tr), *5 tr in next 5ch loop**, tr in next ch (at base of dc); rep from * around, ending last rep at **, sl st in 3rd ch of t-ch—180 (198, 216, 234, 252, 270) tr.

Rnds 2-3: 3ch (counts as tr) skip first st, tr in each tr around, sl st in 3rd ch of t-ch—180 (198, 216, 234, 252, 270) tr. Fasten off at end of last rnd.

Drawstring: Make chain of desired length to fit around waist plus 30.5 cm. Thread Drawstring through the sts in Rnd 2 of Waistband and tie each end of Drawstring in an overhand knot to secure.

DECORATIVE HEM

STITCH KEY

⬯ = chain (ch)

• = slip st (sl st)

✕ = double crochet (dc)

𝐓 = treble crochet (tr)

🔔 = picot

Lacy Patterns and a Pineapple

LACY PATTERNS AND A PINEAPPLE

WHILE CROCHET DEVELOPED IN IMITATION OF OTHER FORMS OF LACE-making, the openwork stitch patterns I've grouped in this chapter don't appear to mimic traditional lace. Rather, they exhibit an exploration of the medium of crochet itself. Once you move beyond solid rows of single crochet or regulated rows of mesh, the majority of crochet stitch patterns can be described as lacy. An incredible variety of openwork patterns can be created by combining chains with taller stitches. Armed with a few crochet stitch dictionaries that preserve the efforts of decades of crocheters, I searched for standouts. I found myself attracted to somewhat angular, geometric patterns. I sought those with arched and staggered motifs, with an oblique but rounded quality, like an Art Deco Erté print. Or, come to think of it, like the crown of a pineapple.

The pineapple is such a favorite crochet motif that it can be seen as a category in itself. Pineapples, which were brought to Renaissance Europe from the Caribbean, caused quite a sensation among nobility and began to appear in art and as decorative motifs that symbolized hospitality. As finials—carved decorations atop gables, spires, and other pieces of architecture—pineapples were used by Christopher Wren and other architects instead of the classical Roman pinecones. As the name *pineapple* suggests, the fruit's globe is similar to the pinecone, but the leaves provide so much more flourish. In colonial America, there was passion both for the rare fruit itself and for pineapple-shaped jellies, cakes, ceramics, tableware, and textiles—and later, in crochet designs. Knowing there was such a rich history, I swatched several variations. I found that often one pineapple's base abuts another's top, making for a crowded arrangement, and that the leaves are represented as pressed into the fruit's globe. This annoyed me, so I invented my own pineapple stitch presented here on another item of Caribbean origin, the hammock.

For these projects, I experimented with diverse yarns to come up with exceptional textural renderings, from slinky nylon cord for a purse to fuzzy kid mohair for a blouse, and from delicate cobweb wool socks to the hefty hemp hammock.

fuzzy zigzag blouse

This zigzag pattern reminds me of the meandering geometric lines I'm constantly doodling while talking on the phone. The gossamer kid mohair and silk blend yarn makes a softly draped fabric unexpected in crochet. The glimmering Lurex shoulder panels in dense single crochet appear almost as if studded with glass beads, like the shimmering bead crochet popularized by the flappers of the Jazz Age. The midnight blue colour is a tribute to one of my favorite novels, *Good Morning, Midnight* by Jean Rhys, but it would also be smashing in the gold or pewter colorways available in these yarns.

>> See pattern on page 68.

zipper bling purse

Anyone who's seen my knitting book, titled *Loop-d-Loop*, knows I love zippers. For that collection, I designed a sweater, dissected by multiple separating zippers, that converts to a bolero as you zip off the components. When I found these crystal-studded separating zippers, I just couldn't resist using them for this girlie handbag. Unzipped, the sparkling teeth resemble beaded trim. The shoulder strap zipper separates to form handles, and each side pouch zips off so you can take just the necessities for a quick latte run.

>> See pattern on page 72.

staggered web lacy top

This delicate top was inspired by a vintage crochet bra in mercerized cotton thread that my father sent me. It was among a batch of doilies he got at a flea market along the banks of the Mississippi. At first sight, the V of its neckline didn't help me to discern it was an abbreviated camisole—it looked like a component of something larger set aside unfinished. But it had a worn-in look and traces of ribbon, tattered and faded, running under what I soon recognized as the bust and along the neck edges. It recalled a picture of a 1920s crocheted bra in *Donna Kooler's Encyclopedia of Crochet*. I chose lace-weight merino for my top, as I find it flexible to work with and luxurious to touch, but those in more tropical climates can substitute cotton thread if preferred.

>> See pattern on page 74.

knotwork socks

What sweeps many a knitter into sock fanaticism—and I can speak from experience here—is the joy of forming a three-dimensional object streamlined to the contours of the foot. Countless knitted socks have been held aloft fresh from the needles as the maker smiles broadly in amazement at the simplicity of the engineering. With this in mind, I wondered if sock fanatics existed among crocheters. I found an entire book on crocheted socks, but to my disappointment only a few of the pairs looked fine enough to put into a shoe, with most bordering on slippers. Was it unfeasible to create crochet lacy but strong and flexible enough to hold its shape around the leg?

I charged my friend Ina with the task of implementing such socks. After having one sample worked from toe up, I realized it would be much more flattering to turn the pattern on its side to emphasize the vertical lines, working the sock from the back seam around. Stuck in the gridlock of New York City traffic on the way to the yarn shop, Ina and I debated ways to shape the calves. At the photo shoot, Ina put the final rows on the heels while the model, a dancer with Rebecca Kelly Company, stood by. We think it looks just as great *en pointe* here as hung on the wash line on page 143.

>> See pattern on page 76.

pineapple hammock

Central and South Americans have been sleeping in hammocks for more than a thousand years. Hammocks were an important trade item among native peoples, and their use spread along trade routes, with many styles of woven cloth and ropework evolving. First brought to Europe by Columbus, hammocks became popular among sailors, as they were an ergonomic way to sleep on the shifting sea. For a time, they were even used as space-saving prison bunks in Britain and were a fad in the United States in the 1880s. Here, I've made a hammock emblazoned with another craze from the tropics—pineapples.

>> See pattern on page 79.

fuzzy zigzag blouse

OVERVIEW

Back and Front are worked in lace pattern from Hem to Top; shoulder pieces are worked in dc in Lurex yarn and front and back are gathered in shoulder pieces.

BACK

With MC, work 134 (146, 158, 170, 182) ch.

Foundation Row: Dc in 2nd ch from hook, *5ch, skip next 5ch, dc in next ch; rep from * across, turn—22 (24, 26, 28, 30) 5ch loops made.

Work even in Zigzag String Pattern until Back measures 15.2 cm from beg, ending with Row 5 of patt.

Shape Sides

Inc Row: 1ch, dc in first dc, 7ch, skip next 2ch space, dc in next dc, *7ch, skip next 5ch loop, dc in next dc; rep from * across, ending with 7ch, skip next 2ch space, dc in last dc, turn—23 (25, 27, 29, 31) 7ch loops made (1 loop inc made). *(Note: This row is now equivalent to Row 2 of patt.)*

Rep Rows 3–5 of patt.

Rep last 4 rows 3 times—26 (28, 30, 32, 34) 7ch loops at end of last 7ch row.

Cont to work even in patt until piece measures approx 33 cm from beg, ending with a Row 1 of patt (for straight edge). Fasten off.

Shape Armhole

Next Row: With RS facing, skip first 2 5ch loops, join MC in next dc, 1ch, dc

---

To fit with about 7.6 cm ease

Shown in second size

MEASUREMENTS

Bust 88.9 (94, 101.6, 109.2, 114.3) cm

Waist 73.7 (83.8, 88.9, 94, 101.6) cm [without being belted]

Length 54.6 (55.9, 58.4, 61, 62.2) cm

YARN

Rowan "Kidsilk Haze" (70% super kid mohair/30% silk) lace weight yarn

6 (6, 7, 7, 8) balls (1 oz/ 25 g; 229 yd/210 m) #585 nightly (MC)

Rowan Lurex "Shimmer" (80% viscose/30% polyester) lace weight yarn

2 balls (1 oz/25 g; 229 yd/210 m) in #339 midnight (CC)

HOOK

2.75 mm (US steel 1) or size to match gauge

NOTIONS

Two 1.9 cm D-rings for Belt Buckle

GAUGE

With MC, 6 5ch loops (in Row 1 of patt) and 24 rows = 10.2 cm in Zigzag String Pattern

With CC, 28 sts = 10.2 cm; 36 rows dc = 10.2 cm.

Always check and MATCH gauge for best results.

in same dc, *7ch, skip next 5ch loop, dc in next dc; rep from * across to within last 2 5ch loops, turn, leaving rem 2 loops unworked—22 (24, 26, 28, 30) 5ch loops made.

Next Row: Rep patt Row 3–22 (24, 26, 28, 30) 7ch loops made.

Next Row: Sl st to centre of first 7ch loop, dc over 2 7ch loops in previous 2 rows, *5ch, dc over next 2 7ch loops in previous 2 rows; rep from * to last 7ch loop, turn, leaving rem sts unworked—21 (23, 25, 27, 29) 7ch loops (1 loop decrease made). *(Note: this row is now equivalent to Row 8 of patt.)*

Starting with Row 1 of patt, work even in patt until Back measures 16.5 (17.8, 20.3, 22.9, 24) cm from beg of armhole shaping. Fasten off.

FRONT

Work same as Back until Front measures approx 7.6 (7.6, 10.2, 12.7, 12.7) cm from beg of armhole shaping, ending with Row 7 of patt.

LEFT FRONT

Next Row: 1ch, dc in first dc, *5ch, dc over next 2 7ch loops in previous 2 rows; rep from * 9 (10, 11, 12, 13) times, 2ch, tr in next (centre) dc, turn, leaving rem sts unworked—10 (11, 12, 13, 14) 5ch loops made plus 2ch space at neck edge.

Row 1: 1ch, dc in first tr, 2ch, skip next 2ch space, dc in next dc, *5ch, skip next 5ch loop, dc in next dc; rep from * across, turn—10 (11, 12, 13, 14) 5ch loops made plus 2ch space at neck edge.

Row 2: Work in Row 2 of patt, ending with 3ch, tr in last dc, turn—10 $\frac{1}{2}$ (11 $\frac{1}{2}$, 12 $\frac{1}{2}$, 13 $\frac{1}{2}$, 14 $\frac{1}{2}$) reps.

Row 3: 1ch, dc in first tr, 3ch, dc in next dc, *7ch, skip next 7ch loop, dc in next dc; rep from * across, turn—10 $\frac{1}{2}$ (11 $\frac{1}{2}$, 12 $\frac{1}{2}$, 13 $\frac{1}{2}$, 14 $\frac{1}{2}$) reps.

Row 4: 5ch (counts as tr, 2ch), dc over next 2 7ch loops in previous 2 rows, joining them together, *5ch, dc

special stitches

ZIGZAG STRING PATTERN
(multiple of 6 plus 1, plus 1 for t-ch)

Foundation Row: Dc in 2nd ch from hook, *5ch, skip next 5ch, dc in next ch; rep from * across, turn.

Row 1 (WS): 1ch, dc in first dc, *5ch, skip 5ch loop, dc in next dc; rep from * across, turn.

Row 2: 1ch, dc in first dc, *7ch, skip next 5ch loop, dc in next dc; rep from * across, turn.

Row 3: 1ch, dc in first dc, *7ch, skip next 7ch loop, dc in next dc; rep from * across, turn.

Row 4: 5ch (counts as tr, 2ch), dc over next 2 7ch loops in previous 2 rows, joining them together, *5ch, dc over next 2 7ch loops in previous 2 rows; rep from * across to last 7ch loop, 2ch, tr in last dc, turn.

Row 5: 1ch, dc in first tr, 2ch, skip next 2ch space, dc in next dc, *5ch, skip next 5ch loop, dc in next dc; rep from * across to t-ch, 2ch, skip next 2 ch of t-ch, dc in next ch, turn.

Row 6: 6ch (counts as tr, 3ch), skip next 2ch space, dc in next dc, *7ch, skip next 5ch loop, dc in next dc; rep from * across, ending with 3ch, skip next 2ch space, tr in last dc, turn.

Row 7: 1ch, dc in first tr, 3ch, skip next 3ch loop, dc in next dc, *7ch, skip next 7ch loop, dc in next dc; rep from * across, ending with 3ch, skip next 3 ch of t-ch, dc in next ch, turn.

Row 8: 1ch, dc in first dc, *5ch, dc over next 2 7ch loops in previous 2 rows; rep from * ending last rep with dc in last dc, turn.

Rep Rows 1–8 for patt.

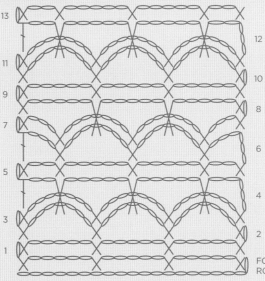

STITCH KEY
⬯ = chain (ch)
✕ = double crochet (dc)

REDUCED SAMPLE OF ZIGZAG STRING PATTERN

over next 2 7ch loops in previous 2 rows; rep from * across, ending with dc in last dc, turn—10 1/2 (11 1/2, 12 1/2, 13 1/2, 14 1/2) reps.

Row 5: 1ch, dc in first dc, *5ch, skip next 5ch loop, dc in next dc; rep from * across to t-ch, 2ch, skip next 2 ch of t-ch, dc in next ch, turn—10 1/2 (11 1/2, 12 1/2, 13 1/2, 14 1/2) reps.

Row 6: 6ch (counts as tr, 3ch), skip next 2ch space, dc in next dc, *7ch, skip next 5ch loop, dc in next dc; rep from * across, ending with dc in last dc, turn—10 1/2 (11 1/2, 12 1/2, 13 1/2, 14 1/2) reps.

Row 7: 1ch, dc in first dc, *7ch, skip next 7ch loop, dc in next dc; rep from * across, ending with 3ch, skip next 3 ch of t-ch, dc in next ch, turn—10 1/2 (11 1/2, 12 1/2, 13 1/2, 14 1/2) reps.

Row 8: 1ch, dc in first dc, *5ch, dc over next 2 7ch loops in previous 2 rows; rep from * ending with 2ch, tr in last dc, turn—10 1/2 (11 1/2, 12 1/2, 13 1/2, 14 1/2) reps.

Rep last 8 rows until Left Front measures same as finished Back. Fasten off.

RIGHT FRONT

Foundation Row: With RS facing, join MC in centre dc of Front, 5ch (counts as tr, 2ch), dc over next 2 7ch loops in previous 2 rows, *5ch, dc over next 2 7ch loops in previous 2 rows; rep from *; rep from * across, ending with dc in last st, turn.

Work even in est patt on 10 1/2 (11 1/2, 12 1/2, 13 1/2, 14 1/2) reps same as Left Front, reversing all shaping.

BACK SHOULDER PIECE

With CC, work 99 (107, 115, 127, 135) ch.

Row 1 (RS): Dc in 2nd ch from hook, dc in each ch across, turn—98 (106, 114, 126, 134) dc.

Rows 2–4: 1ch, dc in each dc across, turn—98 (106, 114, 126, 134) dc.

Row 5: Sl st in each of first 3 (4, 4, 4, 4) sts, 1ch, dc in same st, dc in each st across to within last 2 (3, 3, 3, 3) sts, turn, leaving rem sts unworked—94 (100, 108, 120, 128) dc.

Dec 3 sts at each end of next 0 (2, 3, 9, 13) rows, then dec 2 sts at each end of next 13 (11, 10, 4, 0) rows—42 (44, 50, 50, 50) sts rem at end of last row. Fasten off.

LEFT FRONT SHOULDER PIECE

With CC, work 50 (54, 58, 64, 68) ch.

Row 1 (RS): Dc in 2nd ch from hook, dc in each ch across, turn—49 (53, 57, 63, 67) dc.

Row 2: 1ch, dc in each dc across, turn—49 (53, 57, 63, 67) dc.

Shape Neck Edge

Row 3: 1ch, dc in each dc across to within last 8 sts, turn, leaving rem sts unworked—41 (45, 49, 55, 59) dc.

Row 4: Sl st in each of first 4 sts, 1ch, dc in same st, dc in each dc across, turn.

Starting with Row 5 of Back Shoulder Piece patt, shape shoulder same as Back, at the same time, dec 3 sts at neck edge on next 0 (1, 2, 2, 2) rows, then dec 2 sts at neck edge on next 5 (4, 4, 4, 4) rows, then cont to work shoulder shaping as est on Back, working even at neck edge—0 sts rem at end of last row.

RIGHT FRONT SHOULDER PIECE

Work same as Left Shoulder Piece, reversing shaping.

SLEEVES (make 2)

Sleeve Cap: Starting at top edge, with MC, work 50 (56, 62, 68, 74) ch.

Foundation Row (worked as Row 5 of patt): Dc in 2nd ch from hook, 2ch, skip next 2 ch, dc in next ch, *5ch, skip 5ch, dc in next ch; rep from * across to within last 3 ch, 2ch, skip next 2 ch, dc in last ch, turn—7 (8, 9, 10, 11) 5ch loops.

Inc Row: 1ch, dc in first st, 7ch, skip next 2ch space, dc in next dc, *7ch, skip next 5ch loop, dc in next dc; rep from * across, ending with 7ch, skip next 2ch space, dc in last dc, turn—9 (10, 11, 12, 13) 7ch loops made. *(Note: This row is now equivalent to Row 2 of patt.)*

Rep Rows 3–5 of patt.

Rep Inc Row—10 (11, 12, 13, 14) 7ch loops made.

Rep last 4 rows 6 times—16 (17, 18, 19, 20) 7ch loops at end of last row.

Work even in patt until Sleeve Cap measures 12.7 (12.7, 15.2, 15.2, 17.8) cm from beg, ending with Row 8 of patt. Do not fasten off.

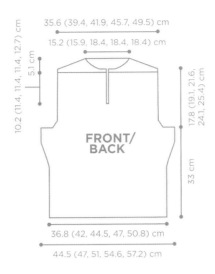

35.6 (39.4, 41.9, 45.7, 49.5) cm
15.2 (15.9, 18.4, 18.4, 18.4) cm
5.1 cm
10.2 (11.4, 11.4, 11.4, 12.7) cm
17.8 (19.1, 21.6, 24.1, 25.4) cm
33 cm
FRONT/ BACK
36.8 (42, 44.5, 47, 50.8) cm
44.5 (47, 51, 54.6, 57.2) cm

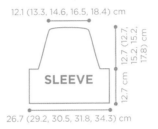

12.1 (13.3, 14.6, 16.5, 18.4) cm
12.7 (12.7, 15.2, 15.2, 17.8) cm
12.7 cm
SLEEVE
26.7 (29.2, 30.5, 31.8, 34.3) cm

Shape Underarm

Drop loop from hook to be picked up later. Join a separate strand of MC at end of last row, ch 12. Fasten off strand.

Next Row: Pick up dropped loop at end of last row, ch 13, dc in 2nd ch from hook, (5ch, skip next 5ch, dc in next ch) twice, work in patt of Row 1 across Sleeve, (5ch, skip next 5ch, dc in next ch) twice across ch-12, turn—20 (21, 22, 23, 24) 5ch loops made.

Work even in est patt until Sleeve measures 12.7 cm from beg of Underarm shaping, ending with Row 4 of patt. Fasten off.

FINISHING

With RS of Back and Back Shoulders together, join MC at one side, 1ch, working through double thickness, dc evenly across, easing in the lighter fabric of body to stiffer shoulder pieces. Join Shoulder pieces to each

Front in same manner. With CC, sew shoulder seams. With MC sew side seams and sleeve seams. Set in Sleeves, easing in fullness.

PLACKET TRIM

Row 1: With RS facing, join CC at top of Left Front neck opening, 1ch, dc evenly down Left Front edge, then dc evenly up Right Front neck edge. Fasten off.

SLEEVE TRIM

Rnd 1: With RS facing, join CC in first 5ch loop in 4th row up from bottom edge, 1ch, work 3 dc in each 5ch loop around adding or subtracting sts for desired fit, sl st in first dc to join. Fasten off. Rep Sleeve Trim around other Sleeve.

COLLAR

Row 1: With RS facing, join MC in first st on neck edge of Right Shoulder piece, 1ch, dc in same st, *7ch, skip next approx 3 sts (approx 1.3 cm) dc in next st; rep from * across neck edge, ending with dc in last st on neck edge of Left Shoulder piece, turn.

Row 2: Work in Row 3 of patt across, turn.

Row 3: Work in Row 4 of patt across. Fasten off.

BELT

With CC make a ch 10.2 cm longer than wearer's waist.

Row 1: Dc in 2nd ch from hook, dc in each ch across, turn.

Rows 2–4: 1ch, dc in each dc across, turn. Fasten off.

D-RING COVER (make 2)

Rnd 1: Join CC in one D-ring, 1ch, work dc in D-ring to fill, sl st in first dc join.

Place D-rings at one end of belt, fold 1.3 cm of belt end over flat edge of D-rings and sew in place.

zipper bling purse

OVERVIEW

Pouches and purse are each made in one piece. Nylon cord is slippery and tends to fray—apply Fray Check to ends to counteract.

SIDE POUCH (make 2)

Top Front of Pouch: Starting at top edge, work 39ch (6 6-st reps plus 1, plus 2 for t-ch). Work in Acrobat Stitch until 9 rows have been completed.

Shape Pouch Bottom: Row 10: Sl st to 10th st (centre tr of first complete shell), 2ch (counts as tr), skip first 3 tr, (3 tr, 3ch, 3 tr) in each of next 4 4ch loops, skip next 2 tr, tr in next tr, turn, leaving rem sts unworked (1 shell decrease on each end).

Back of Pouch: Starting with Row 3 of patt, cont in patt over 4 reps as established, working 9 rows total from Bottom shaping.

With RS facing, fold pouch with bottom edge aligned with top edge for top opening, join yarn 4 sts in from edge at pouch bottom shaping row, 1ch, working through double thickness of sides, dc Front to Back. Rep on other side of Pouch.

PURSE

Starting at bottom edge, work 129ch (21 6-st reps plus 1, plus 2 for t-ch).

Work in Acrobat Stitch until 11 rows have been completed. Fasten off.

With RS facing, fold Purse in half, matching sts across sides, join yarn at top corner, 1ch, working through double thickness of sides, dc across side seam. Fasten off.

MEASUREMENTS

17.8 cm deep x 38.1 cm wide

YARN

J&P Coats "Crochet Nylon" (100% nylon) cabled cord
3 spools (4.7 oz/133 g; 150 yd/137 m) in #52 pink

HOOK

3.25 mm (US D/3)
or size to match gauge

NOTIONS

2 black separating zips 12.7 cm with crystal teeth (Daytona Trimming)

1 black separating zip 48.3 cm with crystal teeth for handle

15.2 cm length of nylon tape (2.5 cm wide) (to attach zip handle)

1 metre black satin fabric for inner lining

1 metre black/silver metallic mesh fabric for outer lining

Sewing needle and strong thread (sewing machine optional)

5 black metal snaps 1.9 cm

Fray Check

GAUGE

4 patt reps (3 shells in Row 2) and 7 rows = 10.2 cm in Acrobat stitch pattern

Always check and MATCH gauge for best results.

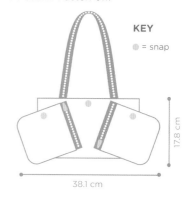

KEY

⬤ = snap

17.8 cm

38.1 cm

BOTTOM EDGING

Turn Purse RS out, with Front facing, matching sts across foundation ch on bottom edge, working through double thickness, join yarn in first ch, 1ch, dc in each ch across to side. Fasten off.

FINISHING

Pouch Assembly: Using pouch as template, cut one piece of each fabric twice as deep as pouch, adding 1.6 cm seam allowance on all sides. With RS of 2 pieces of fabric together, leaving top edge open, sew 3 sides of lining. Turn lining RS out. Fold seam allowance on top edges to inside of resulting "bag" and press. With mesh fabric to outside and satin on inside, fold bag in half with bottom edge meeting top folded edge. Invisibly whip stitch edges together. Place lining in Pouch with opening in front. With top of one 12.7 cm zip to the left, insert left selvedge of zip between the 2 layers of fabric at front of lining. Sew top edge of lining around top opening of pouch, with zip sandwiched in between 2 layers of fabric. Assemble 2nd Pouch in same way.

PURSE ASSEMBLY

Assemble Zip Handle: Place 4 markers on top edge of purse, positioned 7.6 cm to the left and to the right of centre on both front and back. Place 48.3 cm zip to WS of top opening of Purse with zip pull (top) at right marker, and base at left marker. At zip pull end of zip tape, sew one side

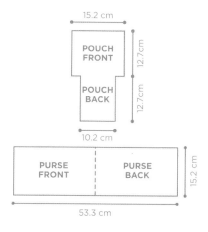

special stitches

ACROBAT STITCH (work a multiple of 6ch plus 1, plus 2 for tch)

Row 1 (RS): 2 tr in 3rd ch from hook, *4ch, skip next 5ch, 5 tr in next ch; rep from * across, ending with 3 tr in last ch, turn.

Row 2: 2ch (counts as tr), skip first 3 tr, (3 tr, 3ch, 3 tr) in each 4ch loop across to last 4ch loop, skip next 2 tr, tr in top of t-ch, turn.

Row 3: 6ch (counts as trtr, 1ch), skip first 4 tr, (5 tr, 4ch) in each 3ch loop across to last 3ch loop, 1ch, trtr in top of t-ch, turn.

Row 4: 5ch (counts as tr, 1ch), 3 tr in next 1ch space, (3 tr, 3ch, 3 tr) in each 4ch loop across to last 4ch loop, (3 tr, 1ch, tr) in t-ch, turn.

Row 5: 2ch (counts as tr), 2 tr in next 1ch space, 4ch, (5 tr, 4ch) in each 3ch space across to last 3ch loop, 3 tr in t-ch, turn.

Rep Rows 2–5 for patt.

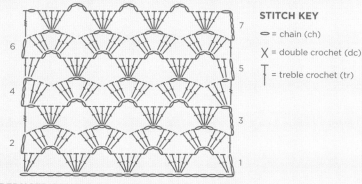

STITCH KEY

⬯ = chain (ch)

X = double crochet (dc)

T = treble crochet (tr)

REDUCED SAMPLE OF ACROBAT STITCH PATTERN

of tape to WS at back of Purse and other side to WS at front of Purse.

Zip Tabs: Fold one 7.6 cm length of nylon tape lengthwise and sew both layers to WS of purse at front left purse marker. Sew 2nd folded piece of tape to WS at left back marker. Trim each to 2.5 cm. Separate zip and enfold each side bottom edge of zip tape in the corresponding Zip Tab and sew in place, being careful not to interfere with zip function.

Purse Lining: Make and join Purse Lining same as for Pouch Linings, using Purse as a template.

FINISHING

Place each Pouch (with zip zipped up but attached to front edge only) on front of purse at a 20-degree angle so that bottom of pouch roughly meets bottom corners of purse, placing top of zips at markers on top edge of Purse and bottom of zips 6.4 cm apart at bottom of Purse. Sew the unattached zip tape to purse working through crochet and mesh layers on front of Purse but not through satin lining. When unzipped the pouch should detach with half of zip tape remaining as a decorative trim on Purse.

Sew one half of one snap to WS of Purse, centered on top front edge. Sew other half on inside back edge to correspond. Sew one half of one snap to back of one pouch, approximately 2.5 cm below top fold. Sew other half of snap to corresponding position on front of Purse. Sew remaining snap to 2nd Pouch in same manner.

staggered web lacy top

Fabric is stretchy. For a close-fitting garment, allow 0 to 2.5 cm ease at bust.

Shown in smallest size

MEASUREMENTS
Waist/Bust under breast 83.8 (92.7, 101.6, 109.2) cm *(Note: Upper pieces form breast covering)*
Length 52.7 (55.2, 57.2, 59.1) cm

YARN
Morehouse Farm "Lace" (100% merino wool) fingering weight yarn
5 (5, 6, 6) hanks (1 oz/28 g; 220 yd/201 m) in aster

HOOKS
2.75 mm (US steel 1) or size needed to obtain gauge

NOTIONS
1.5 (1.75, 2, 2.25) metre cotton

lace ribbon (with centre eyelets to weave drawstring through) 1 cm wide for drawstring casing and trim
Sewing needle and thread to match ribbon

GAUGE
34 sts (3 reps) = 12.7 cm; 10 rows = 10.2 cm in Staggered Web Stitch Pattern.
Always check and MATCH gauge for best results.

OVERVIEW

Blouse is constructed in four pieces: two identical top pieces A and B are worked to be placed sideways over the bust and shoulders with foundation rows forming neckline and final rows forming sleeves of sorts; front (C) and back (D) pieces are worked from top down to be joined to A and B just below bust on front and just below shoulders at back.

RIGHT AND LEFT FRONT

Pieces A and B (make 2 identical to be arranged in opposing directions as shown)

Make 79 (90, 101, 112) ch, work in Staggered Web Stitch Pattern (7 [8, 9, 10] reps in row) until piece measures 16.5 (21, 23.5, 25.4) cm from beg. Fasten off and set aside.

BOTTOM FRONT

Piece C: Make 110 (123, 134, 145) ch, work in Staggered Web Stitch Pattern (10 [11, 12, 13] reps in row) until piece measures 27.9 cm from beg. Fasten off and set aside.

BACK

Piece D: Make 90 (101, 112, 123) ch, work in Staggered Web Stitch Pattern (8 [9, 10, 11] reps in row) until piece measures 15.2 cm from beg. Drop loop from hook and hold st with safety pin.

Shape Armholes: Join a separate strand of yarn at beg of last row, 11ch, fasten off. Pick up dropped loop, 12ch.

Next Row: Dc in 2nd ch from hook, 2ch, skip next 2 ch, tr in each of next 2 ch, 2ch, skip next 2 ch, dc in each of next 5 sts, 2ch, tr in same tr, *(1ch, skip next tr, tr in next tr) twice, 1ch, tr in next 1ch space, skip next 2 1ch spaces**, 5 tr in next 2ch space, 2ch, tr in next tr; rep from * across, ending last rep at **, 4 tr in last 2ch space of t-ch, tr in 3rd ch of t-ch, 2ch, skip next 2 ch, tr in each of next 2 ch, 2ch, skip next 2 ch, dc in each of last 5ch, turn—10 (11, 12, 13) reps established.

Cont in Staggered Web Stitch Pattern until piece measures 33 cm from beg of shaping. Fasten off and set aside.

FINISHING

Arrange side edges of Pieces A and B at foundation row (straight edge) of Piece C, so that their straight edges point into neck and scalloped edges point outward as shown on diagram, and there is about 2.5 cm space open at centre of Piece C. Sew, easing top pieces along Piece C.

Take up Piece D with scalloped edge pointing downward, and align hem to hem with Piece C, sew side seams to top of Piece C, then continuing seam about 5.1 cm along scalloped edge of Piece A and Piece B. Leaving 18.4 (20.3, 20.3, 21) cm at centre of Piece D open for back neck, sew next 7.6 (8.9, 10.8, 12.7) cm of left shoulder to corresponding section of edge of Piece A; sew the rem length of Piece A edge down side of piece D to form sleeve cap. Sew Piece B to right shoulder and armhole of Piece D in same manner.

FRONT/NECK TRIM

Prepare ribbon for Trim: Cut a 4-m length of yarn for drawstring. Fold yarn length in half and weave through eyelets of lace ribbon, leaving an equal amount of yarn on each end of ribbon. Leaving extra yarn free for drawstring, arrange and pin assembled Trim with picots facing

special stitches

STAGGERED WEB STITCH PATTERN

(Pattern uses a foundation ch with a multiple of 11 sts plus 1 + 1 for t-ch. For gauge swatch, work ch 35.

Row 1 (RS): Dc in 2nd ch from hook, *2ch, skip next 2 ch, tr in each of next 2 ch, 2ch, skip next 2 ch, dc in each of next 5ch; rep from * across, turn.

Row 2: 5ch (counts as tr, 2ch), tr in first dc, *(1ch, skip next dc, tr in next dc) twice, 1ch, tr in next 2ch space, skip next 2 tr**, 5 tr in next 2ch space, 2ch, tr in next dc; rep from * across, ending last rep at **, 4 tr in last 2ch space, tr in last dc, turn.

Row 3: 5ch (counts as tr, 2ch), tr in first tr, *(1ch, skip next tr, tr in next tr) twice, 1ch, tr in next 1ch space, skip next 2 1ch spaces**, 5 tr in next 2ch space, 2ch, tr in next tr; rep from * across, ending last rep at **, 4 tr in last 2ch space of t-ch, tr in 3rd ch of t-ch, turn.

Rep Row 3 for stitch pattern.

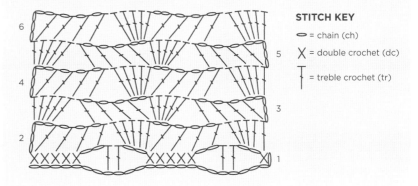

STITCH KEY

⬮ = chain (ch)

X = double crochet (dc)

┬ = treble crochet (tr)

downward starting at left side seam, along foundation row edge of Bottom Front. Sew Trim in place. Arrange another length of prepared Trim around neck edge, beginning and ending at centre Front with picots

of ribbon facing away from edges of work. Sew Trim in place. Sew side edges of ribbon together and tack into junction at centre Front. Pull drawstring ends to adjust fit around bust and neck and secure to WS.

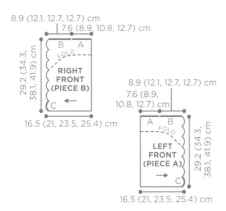

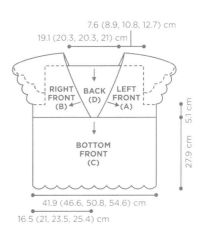

knotwork socks

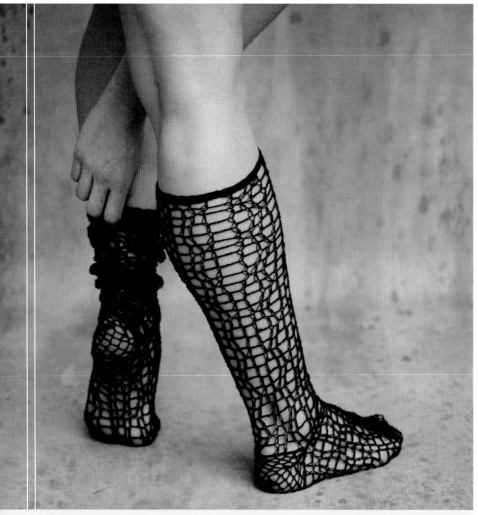

One size. To fit women's shoe sizes 4 1/2–7 1/2. Yarn and stitch pattern are very stretchy.

MEASUREMENTS

Foot: Stretches from 20.3–27.9 cm long; Stretches up to 22.9 cm in circumference

Ankle: Stretches up to 22.9 cm in circumference

Calf: Stretches up to 38.1 cm in circumference

YARN

Jade Sapphire "Lacy Lamb" (100% wool) lace weight yarn

1 ball (1.93 oz/55 g; 825 yd/757 m) in walnut

HOOK

1.5 mm (US steel 8)

NOTIONS

Darning/tapestry needle for seaming

GAUGE

4 sts = 10.2 cm Knot Stitch Pattern; 8 rows = 8.3 cm in foot pattern

Always check and MATCH gauge for best results.

OVERVIEW

Sock is worked sideways in two segments from centre back seam. Length of foot is worked from centre of sole around and cuff is worked around with calf shaping worked in pattern repeat. Toe and heel and cuff edging are worked last in rounds of fishnet.

SOCK (make 2)

FOOT

Make 50ch (3 16-st reps plus 1, plus 1 for t-ch).

Foundation Row (RS): Dc in 2nd ch from hook, *knot st, skip next 3 ch, dtr in next ch, knot st, skip next 3 ch, quad tr in next ch, knot st, skip next 3 ch, dtr in next ch, knot st, skip next 3 ch, dc in next ch; rep from * across, turn—12 knot sts.

Rows 1–22: Work in Knot Stitch Patt, ending with Row 6 of patt.

Row 23: 3ch, dc in 2nd ch from hook, *3ch, skip next knot st, tr in next st; rep from * across, turn. (Note: 3ch loops replace knot sts, to correspond with foundation ch when sewn tog.) Fasten off, leaving a long tail.

Fold Foot in half lengthwise, with RS tog, matching sts in last row with foundation ch, sew with whip stitch (seam runs centre bottom of foot). Turn Foot RS out.

CUFF

(Note: Knot Stitch Pattern is altered by working longer sts at one end of Cuff to make circumference larger around calf.)

special stitches

KNOT STITCH (knot st)
Draw up a loop 1 cm long, yo, draw yarn through long loop on hook (ch made), insert hook in single strand (bottom part) of long loop just made, yo, draw yarn through loop, yo, draw through 2 loops on hook (dc made to complete knot st).

QUAD TREBLE (quad tr)
Yo 4 times, insert hook in next st, yo, draw through st, (yo, draw through 2 loops on hook) 5 times.

KNOT STITCH PATTERN
Make a multiple of 16ch plus 1, plus 1 for t-ch.

Foundation Row (RS): Dc in 2nd ch from hook, *knot st, skip next 3 ch, dtr in next ch, knot st, skip next 3 ch, quad tr in next ch, knot st, skip next 3 ch, dtr in next ch, knot st, skip next 3 ch, dc in next ch; rep from * across, turn.

Row 1: 3ch, dc in 2nd ch from hook, *knot st, skip next knot st, tr in next st; rep from * across, turn.

Row 2: 6ch, dc in 2nd ch from hook, *knot st, skip next knot st, dtr in next st, knot st, skip next knot st, dc in next st, knot st, skip next knot st, dtr in next st, knot st, skip next knot st, quad tr in next st; rep from * across, turn.

Rows 3–4: Rep Rows 1–2.

Row 5: Rep Row 1.

Row 6: 1ch, dc in first st, *knot st, skip next knot st, dtr in next st, knot st, skip next knot st, quad tr in next st, knot st, skip next knot st, dtr in next st, knot st, skip next knot st, dc in next st; rep from * across, turn.

Row 7: Rep Row 1.

Row 8: Rep Row 6.

Rep Rows 1–8 for patt.

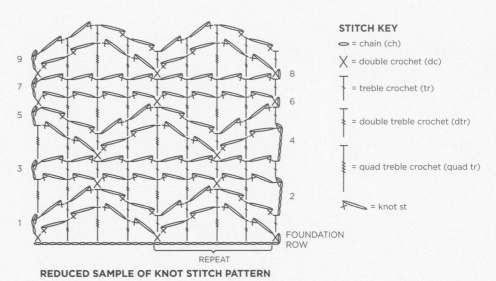

STITCH KEY

⌒ = chain (ch)

X = double crochet (dc)

┬ = treble crochet (tr)

┬ = double treble crochet (dtr)

┬ = quad treble crochet (quad tr)

⟋ = knot st

FOUNDATION ROW

REPEAT

REDUCED SAMPLE OF KNOT STITCH PATTERN

Make 114ch (7 16-st reps plus 1, plus 1 for t-ch).

Dc in 2nd ch from hook, *knot st, skip next 3 ch, dtr in next ch, knot st, skip next 3 ch, quad tr in next ch, knot st, skip next 3 ch, dtr in next ch, knot st, skip next 3 ch, dc in next ch; rep from * across, turn—28 knot sts.

Rows 1–2: Work Rows 1–2 of Knot Stitch Network Pattern.

Row 3 (WS): 6ch, (knot st, skip next knot st, quad tr in next st) 9 times, (knot st, skip next knot st, dtr in next st) 10 times, (knot st, skip next knot st, tr in next stitch) 8 times, turn—28 knot sts.

Rows 4–6: Work Rows 4–6 of Knot Stitch Network Pattern.

Row 7: Rep Row 3 of Cuff.

Row 8: Work Row 8 of Knot Stitch Network Pattern.

Rows 9–16: Rep Rep Rows 1–8 of Cuff.

Rows 17–22: Rep Rep Rows 1–6 of Cuff.

Row 23: 6ch, dc in 2nd ch from hook, (3ch, skip next knot st, quad tr in next st) 9 times, (3ch, skip next knot st, dtr in next st) 10 times, (3ch, skip next knot st, tr in next stitch) 8 times, turn—28 3ch loops. Fasten off, leaving a long tail. Fold Cuff in half lengthwise, with RS tog, matching sts in last row with foundation ch, sew with whip stitch. Turn Cuff RS out.

FINISHING

Attach Foot to Cuff: Joining Row: Place a marker 6 rows to the left and right of back seam on one end of Foot piece. Rep on smaller end of Cuff. With RS of Foot and Cuff tog, matching markers, join yarn in first marked row-end st, working through double thickness of Foot and Cuff, sl st evenly across to next pair of markers. Fasten off, leaving remaining sts unworked for Heel.

HEEL

With RS of Sock facing, join yarn on Heel opening at junction at edge of seam where Foot and Cuff are joined, 1ch, work 80 dc evenly spaced around Heel opening (working into spaces and loops rather than into sts), sl st in first dc to join.

Rnd 1: 1ch, dc in first dc, 4ch, skip next 3 dc, *dc in next dc, 4ch, skip next 3 dc; rep from * around, sl st in first dc to join—20 4ch loops.

Rnd 2: Sl st to centre of first loop, 1ch, dc in first loop, *(4ch, dc) in each of next 9 4ch loops**, dc in next loop; rep from * to ** once, sl st in first dc to join—18 4ch loops.

Rnd 3: Sl st to centre of first loop, 1ch, dc in first loop, *(4ch, dc) in each of next 8 4ch loops**, dc in next loop; rep from * to ** once, sl st in first dc to join—16 4ch loops.

Rnd 4: Sl st to centre of first loop, 1ch, dc in first loop, *(4ch, dc) in each of next 7 4ch loops**, dc in next loop; rep from * to ** once, sl st in first dc to join—14 4ch loops.

Rnd 5: Sl st to centre of first loop, 1ch, dc in first loop, *(4ch, dc) in each of next 6 4ch loops**, dc in next loop; rep from * to ** once, sl st in first dc to join—12 4ch loops.

Rnd 6: Sl st to centre of first loop, 1ch, dc in first loop, *(4ch, dc) in each of next 5 4ch loops**, dc in next loop; rep from * to ** once, sl st in first dc to join—10 4ch loops.

Rnd 7: Sl st to centre of first loop, 1ch, dc in first loop, *(4ch, dc) in each of next 4 4ch loops**, dc in next loop; rep from * to ** once, sl st in first dc to join—8 4ch loops. Fasten off, leaving a sewing length. With WS facing, flatten Heel, horizontally, sew last rnd tog for Heel seam.

TOE

Rnd 1: With RS facing, join yarn at bottom seam on Toe opening of Foot, 1ch, work 56 dc evenly spaced around Toe opening, sl st in first dc to join—56 dc.

Rnd 2: 1ch, dc in first dc, 4ch, skip next 3 dc, *dc in next dc, 4ch, skip next 3 dc; rep from * around, ending with 1ch, htr in first dc instead of last 4ch loop—14 loops.

Rnds 3–12: 1ch, (dc, 4ch) in each loop around, ending with 1ch, htr in first dc instead of last 4ch loop—14 loops. Fasten off, leaving a sewing length. With WS facing, flatten Toe, horizontally, sew last rnd tog for Toe seam.

TOP BAND

(Note: Top Band is worked over a multiple of 4 sts. As written, Top Band will tighten the top edge to approximately 35.6 cm circumference. To adjust circumference, work a multiple of 4 dc around top edge of Cuff in Rnd 1, adjusting to achieve a comfortable fit that will not slide down when worn.)

Rnd 1: With RS facing, join yarn to top of Cuff at back seam, 1ch, work 80 (or a multiple of 4) dc evenly spaced around top edge of Cuff, sl st in first dc to join—80 dc.

Rnd 2: 1ch, dc in first dc, 4ch, skip next 3 dc, *dc in next dc, 4ch, skip next 3 dc; rep from * around, ending with 1ch, htr in first dc instead of last 4ch loop—20 loops.

Rnds 3–4: 1ch, (dc, 4ch) in each loop around, ending with 1ch, htr in first dc instead of last 4ch loop—20 loops. Fasten off.

pineapple hammock

OVERVIEW

Yarn is doubled throughout. The pattern of staggered pineapples is placed symmetrically, with 9 pineapples alternating with 8 pineapples. The pattern has no RS or WS as pineapples alternately begin on odd and even number rows of pattern repeat. *Note: We rigged this hammock with shorter dowels and thus created a cocoon shape much like Mayan hammocks which are traditionally strung up higher, but shot it on a hammock stand designed for a more flat style. If you are planning to use a hammock stand, use a longer dowel to stretch hammock width and prevent it sagging low to ground. You can find a variety of hammock stands and tree wraps online. Most importantly, please review the safety tips at www.hammock-hammocks.com/safety-Stand.htm.*

HAMMOCK BED

With 2 strands of yarn held together as one, ch 226.

Base Edge Row: Dc into 2nd ch from hook, dc in each ch across, turn—225 dc.

Row 1: 3ch (counts as tr), tr in first dc, 2ch, skip next 2 dc, *dc in next dc,

MEASUREMENTS
Width: 152.4 cm
Length: 177.8 cm unstretched (bed, not including area beyond dowels)

YARN
Lanaknits Hemp for Knitting "Allhemp6" (100% long fiber hemp), sportweight yarn

24 hanks (3.25 oz/ 90 g; 150 yd/137 m) in #50 brick
Note: Hemp is strong. If substituting yarn be sure to select a strong fiber that will hold body weight.

HOOK
5.0 mm (US H/8) or size to match gauge

NOTIONS
Two 81.3 cm long wooden dowels with 6 mm diameter
32 yd/30 m rope, cotton with nylon core
2 m heavy gauge chain
Two 7.6 cm metal S hooks

GAUGE
1 pattern repeat (from centre of pineapple to centre of next pineapple) = 17.8 cm; 9 rows in pattern = 17.8 cm tall in pineapple pattern with yarn doubled, slightly stretched

Make 44ch and work gauge swatch following the charted stitch repeat
Always check and MATCH gauge for best results.

special stitches

QUAD TREBLE (quad tr)
Yo (4 times), insert hook in next st, yo, draw yarn through st, (yo, draw yarn through 2 loops on hook) 5 times.

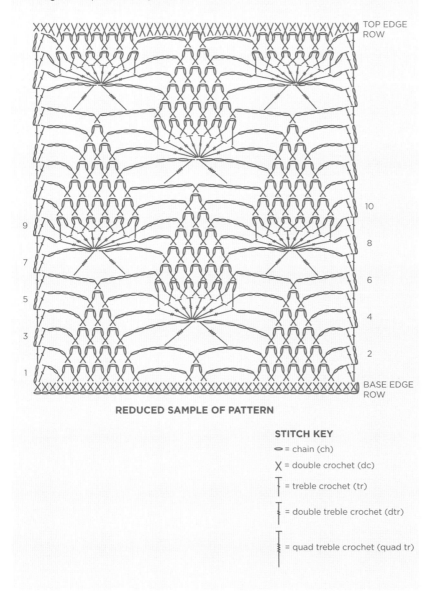

TOP EDGE ROW

10

8

9

7

6

5

4

3

2

1

BASE EDGE ROW

REDUCED SAMPLE OF PATTERN

STITCH KEY

◠ = chain (ch)

X = double crochet (dc)

╀ = treble crochet (tr)

╪ = double treble crochet (dtr)

≢ = quad treble crochet (quad tr)

(3ch, skip next dc, dc in next dc) 5 times**, 6ch, skip 6 dc, dc in next dc, skip next dc, 3ch, dc in next dc, 6ch, skip 6 dc; rep from * across, ending last rep at **, 2ch, skip next 2 dc, 2 tr in last dc, turn—9 pineapples established.

Row 2: 3ch (counts as tr), tr in first tr, 3ch, skip next 2ch space, *dc into next 3ch loop, (3ch, dc) in each of next 4 3ch loops**, 7ch, skip next 6ch loop, dc in next 3ch loop, 7ch, skip next 6ch loop; rep from * across, ending last rep at **, 3ch, skip next (2ch space and tr), 2 tr in top of t-ch, turn.

Row 3: 3ch (counts as tr), tr in first tr, 4ch, skip next 3ch loop, *dc into next 3ch loop, (3ch, dc) in each of next 3 3ch loops**, 6ch, (quad tr in centre ch of next 7ch loop) twice, 6ch; rep from * across, ending last rep at **, 4ch, skip next (3ch loop and tr), 2 tr in top of t-ch, turn.

Row 4: 3ch (counts as tr), tr in first tr, 5ch, skip next 4ch loop, *dc into next 3ch loop, (3ch, dc) in each of next 2 3ch loops**, 4ch, skip next (6ch loop and quad tr), 8 dtr in next quad tr, 4ch; rep from * across, ending last rep at **, 5ch, skip next (4ch loop and tr), 2 tr in top of t-ch, turn—8 new pineapples established bet 9 original pineapples.

Row 5: 3ch (counts as tr), tr in first tr, 6ch, skip next 5ch loop, *dc into next 3ch loop, 3ch, dc in next 3ch loop**, 6ch, skip next (4ch loop and dtr), (dc, 3ch) bet last skipped and next dtr (6 times), dc bet last skipped and next dtr, 6ch; rep from * across, ending last rep at **, 6ch, skip next (5ch loop and tr), 2 tr in top of t-ch, turn.

Row 6: 3ch (counts as tr), tr in first tr, 7ch, skip next 6ch loop, dc into next 3ch loop, *7ch, skip next 6ch loop, dc into next 3ch loop, (3ch, dc) in each of next 5 3ch loops, 7ch, skip next 6ch loop, dc in next 3ch loop; rep from * across, 7ch, skip next (6ch loop and tr), 2 tr in top of t-ch, turn.

Row 7: 3ch (counts as tr), tr in first tr, *6ch, (quad tr in centre ch of next 7ch loop) twice, 6ch**, dc into next 3ch loop, (3ch, dc) in each of next 4 3ch loops; rep from * across, ending last rep at **, skip next tr, 2 tr in top of t-ch, turn.

Row 8: 3ch (counts as tr), tr in first tr, 1ch, *skip next (6ch loop and quad tr), 8 dtr in next quad tr**, 4ch, skip next 6ch loop, dc into next 3ch loop, (3ch, dc) in each of next 3 3ch loops, 4ch; rep from * across, ending last rep at **, 1ch, skip next (1ch space and tr), 2 tr in top of t-ch, turn.

Row 9: 3ch (counts as tr), tr in first tr, 1ch, skip next (1ch space and dtr), *(dc, 3ch) bet last skipped and next dtr (6 times), dc bet last skipped and next dtr**, 6ch, skip next 4ch loop, dc into next 3ch loop, (3ch, dc) in each of next 2 3ch loops, 6ch, skip next 6ch loop; rep from * across, ending last rep at **, 1ch, skip next (1ch space and tr), 2 tr in top of t-ch, turn.

Row 10: 3ch (counts as tr), tr in first tr, 2ch, skip next 1ch space, *dc into next 3ch loop, (3ch, dc) in each of next 5 3ch loops**, 6ch, skip next 6ch loop, dc in next 3ch loop, 3ch, dc in next 3ch loop, 6ch, skip next 6ch loop; rep from * across, ending last rep at **, 2ch, skip next (1ch space and tr), 2 tr in top of t-ch, turn.

Rep rows 2–10 (9 times) or until piece measures 177.8 cm or desired length

(or use 22 hanks yarn), ending Row 10 of pattern.

Top Edge Row: 1ch, dc in each of first 2 tr, dc in next 2ch space, *dc in next dc, (dc in next 3ch loop, dc in next dc) 5 times**, 6 dc in next 6ch loop, dc in next dc, dc in next 3ch loop, dc in next dc, 6 dc in next 6ch loop; rep from * across, ending last rep at **, dc in next 2ch space, dc in each of last 2 sts—225 dc. Do not fasten off.

BORDER
Rnd 1: With yarn doubled, dc evenly around entire edge to reinforce, sl st in first dc to join. Fasten off.

FINISHING/ASSEMBLY
To rig hammock with nylon core or cotton rope on wooden dowels as shown: Prepare 2 wooden dowels, carving a notch (wide enough to cradle the rope) at each end along centre of tip. Cut the rope in half, about 15.2 metres for each side.

First End of Hammock: Lay out hammock with first prepared dowel aligned along top edge and S hook centered about 61–91.4 cm above. You will need to keep S hook steady at this central point and keep rope lengths adjusted so that the dowel lays straight and perpendicular to hook. Take up rope and lay over S hook leaving about 25.4 cm tail. Stretch the rope toward the dowel (about 91.4 cm) and hammock right corner, threading it under dowel. Then, from WS to RS of hammock through corner loop, come back over the dowel up to the S hook. Bring rope back down, threading it under dowel and from WS to RS of hammock through 3ch space of the base row (centered between

pineapples of the first repeat), then come back over the dowel up to the S hook. Cont working in this manner from right to left, wrapping rope through the edge of the hammock into each of the 3ch spaces between pineapples along the edge, then into final loop at the opposite corner and up to the S hook central point—this will form a bundle of rope over the S hook. You might want to pinch the rope together over the dowel to temporarily hold it in place as you continue to wrap the rope over the S hook, dowel, and hammock edge back and forth. To secure all loops bundled in the S hook take the remaining end of rope and wind it tightly around all strands just below the hook, allowing the loops to lay evenly and smoothly in the S hook. Tie the beginning and end of rope into a square knot. Secure the end of the rope by threading it into the final wraps and trim excess. To keep outer edge rope loops from sliding off dowel, secure them by placing bottom strand of loop into end notch on dowel and top strand at front of dowel. Join the pair of strands around dowel by very tightly tying a small length of nylon thread just above dowel, using square knot that will not slip or loosen. To keep all other rope loops from sliding on dowel, at each point where the rope wraps over the dowel, secure each pair of rope strands to itself in the same manner.

Work Second End of Hammock as for First End, threading rope through 3ch spaces centered between pineapples of Row 10.

Spikes, Clusters, Bobbles, and Puffs

SPIKES, CLUSTERS, BOBBLES, AND PUFFS

WHEN I STARTED PERUSING CROCHET STITCH DICTIONARIES, AMONG THE expected lacy treasures I found a variety of dense patterns that utilized raised and tilted groupings of loops. With this family of crochet stitches, the yarn is merely reeled or bundled and not constrained in a small stitch, so the yarn is shown to a great advantage. Have you ever found a gorgeous skein of hand-dyed yarn that, when worked up, became a fabric of tight, flat, speckled mish-mash? With spikes, clusters, bobbles, and puffs, the yarn is practically in its "raw" state, perfect to show off the beauty of handspun and hand-dyed yarns with variegated thickness and striated colouring.

One of the special elements of crafting is knowing that countless women have found solace and even livelihood while working their hands in the very same stitch patterns. When crocheting, I feel like I'm carrying on that history. I can't help wondering who first made a certain configuration with her hook and how it came to have a particular name. For instance, two of the stitch patterns in this chapter appear to have the names of Catholic saints—Marguerite and Catherine. I thought that perhaps *Marguerite* meant "star," as would make sense for a star-shaped stitch pattern, but it means "pearl." So it's more likely the stitch was named by a devotee of the thirteenth-century princess Marguerite of Hungary, who lived as a nun and was canonized because hundreds of miracles were reportedly granted at her tomb. The wheel-like stitch named after Saint Catherine has visual as well as sentimental meaning. Of noble birth and very learned, Catherine was successfully gaining converts to Christianity when she was ordered put to death on a giant wheel, a Roman torture device, by Emperor Maximus in the year 305. When Catherine touched the wheel it miraculously fell apart, so she was beheaded instead.

I would like to believe in the supernatural powers of these women even though a simple life of devout faith of any sort is problematic in our skeptical, modern world. Their stories certainly lend a romantic aura to crochet stitch patterns and the jacket and cape that feature them, respectively. What might be the legends behind the sidesaddle and clover stitches used in other projects featured here? That's something for you to meditate on as you crochet.

sidesaddle cluster pullover and wrap

I was immediately drawn to this pattern of triangular clusters that lean this way and that. Perhaps my fascination came from it being a rather "knitterly" stitch. It has a cross-hatched quality like entrelac (a knitting technique that gives the fabric a woven appearance), and the vertical lines of the pattern are dominant in a way more akin to knitting. Being a devotee of the über-knitting guru Elizabeth Zimmermann, one of my favorite sweater constructions is knit in the round, from the top down, according to a proportional formula she developed. Here I offer a crochet version of such a yoked sweater. The wrap, edged in dramatic bobbles, stands in for sleeves to highlight how the yoke spans the shoulders like a capelet.

The "sidesaddle" clusters almost appear to be leaves running along a vine and, being somewhat literal-minded, I chose a horticultural colored yarn.

>> *See pattern on page 90.*

catherine wheel cape

Catherine Wheel is a very popular crochet stitch pattern, featured in many an afghan and baby sweater—though crochet designer Lily Chin used it in a metallic bikini. The interlocking wheels are fun to execute: The bottom halves of the circles are formed with cluster stitches pulled into a central point, and the upper halves are formed with a fan of treble crochet worked into the same axis. It's enjoyable to see the fabric build as you fill in valleys and pile up anthills with yarn.

For this cape, I've used super-bulky yarn to magnify the stitch, taking it to an extreme scale. In these subdued colors, it resembles a traditional woolen weave, such as houndstooth. The construction is asymmetrical, but the cape is actually based on a standard poncho style, in which a vertical rectangle is seamed to a horizontal rectangle.

>> *See pattern on page 93.*

marguerite jacket

Marguerite stitch, sometimes known as Spike or Star stitch, forms a dense fabric with overlapping spikes pointing in all directions, like a crowding of little stars. The woven appearance of this stitch provoked my vision of a structured, cropped jacket resembling one sewn in silk noile or another high-end decorator fabric.

This sporty yet sophisticated jacket is undeniably an homage to fashion icon, visionary, and innovator Coco Chanel. It has a spare silhouette but rich patterning that recalls drawing-room damasks with the moiré, watermark effect: light-catching, rippled coloring in organic but geometric zebra-like stripes. The hand-dyed yarn I found to achieve this random patterning is rayon recycled from textile factories in South Asia (a portion of the proceeds from its sale benefits women in Nepal).

>> See pattern on page 97.

clover fan jacket

An arched arrangement of puffs, this stitch pattern is at once lacy and full with a folkloric appeal. The bold triangular cutouts lend it a character that I find quite marvelous from a knitter's perspective—there may be some impossibly convoluted way to imitate this with two needles, but why bother? I have engineered this jacket by making use of the scalloped stitch repeat for optimum flounces. The pattern is worked outward from the waistline and from the top of the sleeve cuff. Because much of the yarn is merely bundled into long loops, the fabric has a fluid drape.

The romantic silhouette of this flouncy jacket makes an interesting combination with the crude wood-cut feel of the patterning. It speaks to me of the progression from the Victorian sensibility toward modern art through William Morris, Cézanne, and other European designers' and artists' interest in "primitive" arts and crafts. Shown in tropical orange and urban gray (page 106).

>> See pattern on page 101.

sidesaddle cluster pullover and wrap

OVERVIEW

The pullover is worked in one piece from neck down in rows. Shaping is achieved by changing hook size and adding an extra ch to the stitch pattern. The edges of Yoke will form neck opening, then after leaving stitches unworked at bottom of Yoke to form sleeves, beg of row is shifted so that seam will run down right side.

pullover

YOKE

With H hook and MC, make 122 (132, 132, 142, 142) ch. Work in Sidesaddle Cluster Pattern 1 on 24 (26, 26, 28, 28) patt reps until 6 rows have been completed. With I hook, continue to work in patt for 6 (6, 6, 8, 8) rows. With J hook, continue to work in patt for 2 rows. Fasten off.

Divide for Body/Form Armholes

Fold Yoke in half with end of rows meeting beg of rows. Foundation ch forms neck edge.

Next Row: With RS facing, skip first 14 (16, 16, 17, 17) clusters, join MC in next CL (at the back of right arm-hole), 5 (5, 10, 10, 15) ch for underarm, skip next 4 clusters for armhole, dc in next CL, (3ch, dc4tog in next 3ch loop, 1ch, dc in next CL) 4 (4, 4, 5, 5)

Close-fitting and in stretchy material sized to fit actual bust measurement
Shown in smallest size

MEASUREMENTS

Pullover: Bust 81.3 (91.4, 101.6, 111.8, 121.9) cm

Length 63.5 (63.5, 63.5, 66, 66) cm

Wrap: 50.8 cm wide x 147.3 cm long

YARN

Manos Del Uruguay "Handcrafted Kettle Dyed Pure Wool" (100% corriedale and merino wool) worsted weight yarn

For Pullover: 4 (5, 6, 6, 7) hanks (3.5oz/100g; 135 yd/123 m) in #55 olive (MC)

For Wrap: 4 hanks in #65 wheat (MC), 1 hank in #59 kohl (CC)

HOOKS

For Pullover: 5 mm (US H/8), 5.5 mm (US I/9) and 6 mm (US J/10)

For Wrap: 8 mm (US L/11)

or sizes needed to obtain gauges

NOTIONS

Hanging marker

Tapestry needle

Two 2.5 cm plastic rings for buttons

GAUGE

For Pullover: 3 patt reps = 10.2 cm; 8 rows = 10.2 cm in Pattern 1 with H hook

2 patt reps = 8.9 cm; 7 rows = 10.2 cm in Pattern 1 with I hook

2 patt reps = 10.2 cm; 6 rows = 10.2 cm in Pattern 1 with J hook

2 patt reps = 12.7 cm; 6 rows = 12.7 cm in Pattern 2 with J hook

For Wrap: 2 patt reps = 12.7 cm; 4 rows = 10.2 cm in Pattern 2 with L hook

Always check and MATCH gauge for best results (pattern is tilted so read row gauge carefully).

times to end of row, 1ch, CL in 3ch turning ch loop, 1ch, [do not turn] working in beg of last row of Yoke, dc in next CL, (3ch, dc4tog in next 3ch loop, 1ch, dc in next CL) 2 (3, 3, 3, 3) times, 5 (5, 10, 10, 15) ch for underarm, skip next 4 clusters for armhole, dc in next CL, (3ch, dc4tog in next 3ch loop, 1ch, dc in next CL) 7 (8, 8, 9, 9) times for back, ending with last dc in same CL as joining, turn.

Next Row (WS): 5ch (counts as tr, 2ch), dc in next CL, *(3ch, dc4tog in next 3ch loop, 1ch, dc in next CL) 6 (7, 7, 8, 8) times, 3ch, dc4tog in next 3ch loop, 1ch, (dc in next ch at underarm, 3ch, dc4tog over next 4 ch, 1ch) 1 (1, 2, 2, 3) times, dc in next CL; rep from * once, omitting last dc, tr in next dc of last rnd, turn—16 (18, 20, 22, 24) patt reps made.

Work even in Sidesaddle Cluster Pattern 1 for 9 more rows. Commence Sidesaddle Cluster Pattern 2 working for 12 rows more or desired length. Fasten off.

FINISHING

With WS facing, dc side seam. With dc, seam neck opening 7.6 cm up from base leaving approx 12.7 (12.7, 12.7, 15.2, 15.2) cm open.

BUTTON (make 2)

With I hook, join yarn in plastic ring, 1ch, work 18 dc in ring, slip st in first dc to join. Fasten off, leaving a long tail. Turn base of dc sts at outer rim inward, filling centre of ring. Thread yarn tail in tapestry needle and sew centre opening closed. With rem yarn, sew buttons to left side of neck opening on Rows 3 and 5.

BUTTON LOOP

With H hook, join yarn to neck opening opposite one Button, 1ch, dc on neck edge, ch 10, sl st in first dc to join, work 15 dc in ch-10 loop, sl st in first dc to join, fasten off. Rep Button Loop opposite other Button.

wrap

With L hook and MC, make 50ch. Work even in Sidesaddle Cluster Pattern 2 on 8 patt reps until piece measures 142.2 cm from beg or until MC is used up, ending with an even number of rows.

BOTTOM TRIM

With RS facing and L hook, working across opposite side of foundation ch, join CC in first ch, do not work a turning ch, *5-trtr bobble in first ch, skip next ch, 2 dc in each of next 2 ch, skip next ch; rep from * across, ending with bobble in last ch, fasten off.

TOP TRIM

Rep Bottom Trim as evenly as possible across top edge to match Bottom Trim.

81.3 (88.9, 88.9, 95.3, 95.3) cm

12.7 (12.7, 12.7, 15.2, 15.2) cm

7.6cm

43.2 cm

30.5 (30.5, 35.6, 35.6, 38.1) cm

FRONT AND BACK

BUST

81.3 (91.4, 101.6, 111.8, 121.9) cm

HIPS

101.6 (114.3, 127, 139.7, 152.4) cm

TR4TOG (referred to as CL)
(Yo, insert hook in next st, yo, draw yarn through st, yo, draw yarn through 2 loops on hook) 4 times in designated sts, yo, draw yarn through 5 loops on hook.

5-TRTR BOBBLE
(Yo 3 times, insert hook in next space, yo, draw yarn through st, [yo, draw yarn through 2 loops on hook] 3 times) 5 times in same st, yo, draw yarn through 6 loops on hook.

SIDESADDLE CLUSTER PATTERN 1 (multiple of 5 sts, plus 1, plus 1 for t-ch)
Row 1 (RS): Dc in 2nd ch from hook, *3ch, dc4tog worked across next 4 ch, 1ch, dc in next ch; rep from * across, turn.

Row 2: 5ch, dc in next CL, *3ch, dc4tog in next 3ch loop, 1ch, dc in next CL; rep from * across, ending with tr in last dc, turn.

Row 3: 1ch, skip first tr, dc in next CL, *3ch, dc4tog in next 3ch loop, 1ch, dc in next CL; rep from * across, ending with last dc in 3rd ch of t-ch, turn.

Rep Rows 2–3 for pattern.

SIDESADDLE CLUSTER PATTERN 2 (multiple of 6 sts plus 1, plus 1 for t-ch)
(This pattern, used to widen bottom of sweater, is the same as Sidesaddle Cluster Pattern 1 except with an extra ch after each CL.)
Row 1 (RS): Dc in 2nd ch from hook, *3ch, dc4tog worked across next 4 ch, 2ch, skip next ch, dc in next ch; rep from * across, turn.

Row 2: 5ch, dc in next CL, *3ch, dc4tog in next 3ch loop, 2ch, dc in next CL; rep from * across, ending with tr in last dc, turn.

Row 3: 1ch, skip first tr, dc in next CL, *3ch, dc4tog in next 3ch loop, 2ch, dc in next CL; rep from * across, ending with last dc in 3rd ch of t-ch, turn.

Rep Rows 2–3 for pattern.

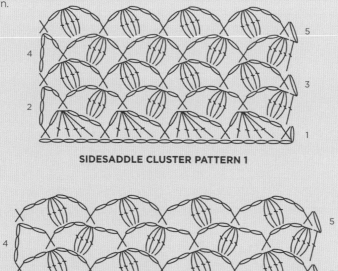

SIDESADDLE CLUSTER PATTERN 1

SIDESADDLE CLUSTER PATTERN 2

STITCH KEY

⌒ = chain (ch)

✕ = double crochet (dc)

┬ = treble crochet (tr)

⋀ or ⦙⦙⦙ = tr4tog

catherine wheel cape

OVERVIEW

Garment consists of two rectangular pieces sewn together in an L-shaped formation: Panel 2 is placed horizontally to cover front to just past centre back (over right shoulder) where its ending row is sewn to side edge of Panel 1 whose length extends over left shoulder and around front. Collar is worked along the shaped side edge of Panel 2.

Alternate 2 rows in each colour as per chart, stranding nonworking yarn loosely up side edge.

PANEL 1

With A, make 27 (37) ch.

Row 1 (RS): Dc in 2nd ch from hook, dc in next ch, *skip next 3 ch, 7 tr in next ch, skip next 3 ch, dc in each of next 3 ch; rep from * across to within last 4 ch, skip 3 ch, 4 tr in last ch, turn.

Drop A to be picked up later, join B to work next 2 rows.

Row 2 (WS): With B, 1ch, dc in each of first 2 tr, *3ch, 7-tr CL worked across next 7 sts, 3ch, dc in each of next 3 tr; rep from * across to within last 4 sts, 3ch, 4-tr CL across last 4 sts, turn.

Row 3: 3ch (counts as tr), 3 tr in first st, *skip next 3ch loop, dc in each of next 3 dc, skip next 3ch loop, 7 tr in next CL; rep from * across to within last 5 sts, skip next 3ch loop, dc in each of last 2 dc, turn.

Drop B to be picked up later, pick up A from 2 rows below to work next 2 rows.

Row 4: With A, 3ch (counts as tr), skip first dc, 3-tr CL worked across

special stitches

CLUSTER (CL)

(Yo, insert hook in next st, yo, draw yarn through st, yo, draw through 2 loops on hook) designated number of times, yo, draw through all loops on hook.

next 3 sts, *3ch, dc in each of next 3 tr, 3ch, 7-tr CL worked across next 7 sts; rep from * across to within last 2 sts, 3ch, dc in next tr, dc in 3rd ch of t-ch, turn.

Row 5: 1ch, dc in each of first 2 dc, *skip next 3ch loop, 7 tr in next CL, skip next 3ch loop, dc in each of next 3 dc; rep from * across to within last 5 sts, skip next 3ch loop and CL, 4 tr in 3rd ch of t-ch, turn.

Drop A, pick up B to work next 2 rows.

Repeat rows 2–5 for pattern, cont to change colors every 2 rows. When piece measures 83.8 (99.1) cm; 22 (26) rows, fasten off.

PANEL 2

Note: First 5 rows of Panel 2 are wider and form a flap.

With B, ch 32 (42).

Row 1 (RS): Dc in 2nd ch from hook, dc in next ch, *skip next 3 ch, 7 tr in next ch, skip next 3 ch**, dc in each of next 3 ch; rep from * across, ending last rep at **, dc in each of last 2 ch, turn.

Drop A to be picked up later, join B to work next 2 rows.

Row 2 (WS): 3ch, skip first dc, 3-tr CL worked across next 3 sts, *3ch, dc in each of next 3 tr, 3ch**, 7-tr CL worked across next 7 sts; rep from * across, ending last rep at **, 4-tr CL worked across last 4 sts, turn.

Row 3: 3ch (counts as tr), 3 tr in first st, *skip next 3ch loop, dc in each of next 3 dc, skip next 3ch loop**, 7 tr in next CL; rep from * across, ending

last rep at **, skip next CL, 4 tr in 3rd ch t-ch, turn.

Drop B to be picked up later, pick up A from 2 rows below to work next 2 rows.

Row 4: 1ch, dc in each of first 2 tr, *3ch, 7-tr CL worked across next 7 sts, 3ch**, dc in each of next 3 tr; rep from * across, ending last rep at **, dc in next tr, dc in 3rd ch of t-ch, turn.

Row 5: 1ch, dc in each of first 2 tr, *skip next 3ch loop, 7 tr in next CL, skip next 3ch loop**, dc in each of next 3 dc; rep from * across, ending last rep at **, dc in each of last 2 dc, turn.

Drop B, pick up A to work next 2 rows.

Row 6: 3ch (counts as tr), skip first dc, 3-tr CL worked across next 3 sts, *3ch, dc in each of next 3 tr, 3ch, 7-tr

CL worked across next 7 sts; rep from * 1 (2) times, 3ch, dc in each of next 2 tr, turn, leaving rem sts unworked (ending at centre of last 7-tr shell of row below).

Row 7: 1ch, dc in each of first 2 dc, *skip next 3ch loop, 7 tr in next CL, skip next 3ch loop, dc in each of next 3 dc; rep from * across to within last 5 sts, skip next 3ch loop and CL, 4 tr in 3rd ch of t-ch, turn.

Drop A, pick up B to work next 2 rows.

Rows 8–11: Maintaining colour sequence as established (2 rows B; 2 rows A), rep Rows 2–5 of Panel 1.

Rep Rows 8–11 until Panel 2 measures 91.4 (106.7) cm from beg (24 [28] rows). Fasten off.

COLLAR

Row 1: With RS facing, working across right side edge of Panel 2, join B with sl st in first st in Row 5 at top of Flap, 3ch (counts as tr), 3 tr in same place, skip next 3 sts of Row 5, dc in next tr, dc in each of next 2 row-end dc (Rows 6 and 7 of Piece 2), *7 tr in top of next row-end CL (Row 8), skip 2 ch of t-ch and dc in next ch (Row 9), dc in each of next

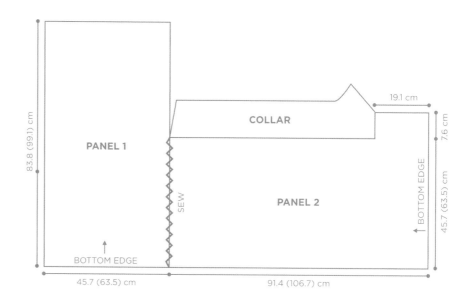

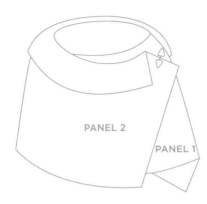

PANEL 2

PANEL 1

2 row-end dc (Rows 10 and 11); rep from * across top edge of Panel 2, ending with 4 tr in top of last row-end tr in row 24 (28), turn.

Drop B to be picked up later, join A to work next 2 rows.

Rows 2–3: With A, rep Rows 4–5 of Panel 2.

Drop A, pick up B to work next row.

Row 4: With B, rep Row 2 of Panel 2. Fasten off.

FINISHING

Trim Row: With RS facing, join A in top left-hand corner of Panel 1, 1ch, working over carried strands of yarn, dc evenly across.

Rep Trim Row across left edge of Panel 2.

Arrange Panels following Construction Diagram. With tapestry needle and B, sew right side edge of Panel 1 to top edge of Panel 2 to base of Collar as shown.

TOGGLE CLOSURE

Drape cape over intended wearer so that collar meets at left shoulder and free end of Panel 1 extends over shoulder to front, to check fit and determine placement of closure.

With sharp leather needle, punch an even number of holes around leather base, place one side on Panel 2 on top edge of flap created by Rows

1–5, sew leather piece to the 4-tr shell in Row 2. Sew other side of toggle to unfinished edge of Panel 1 approx 33 (45.7) cm from final row or determined best placement on left shoulder.

With tapestry needle and B, sew flap edge (Rows 1–5 of Panel 2) to right edge of Panel 1 where Panels meet so that side edges of Collar stand up.

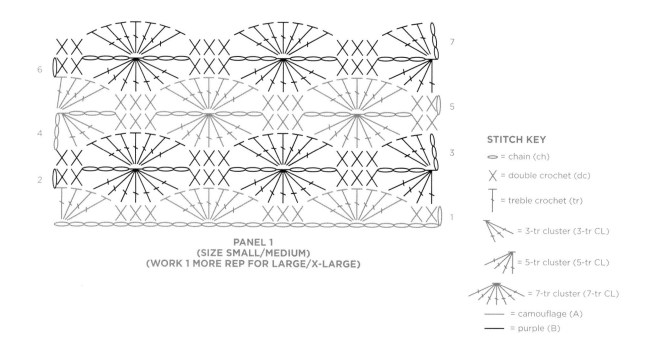

**PANEL 1
(SIZE SMALL/MEDIUM)
(WORK 1 MORE REP FOR LARGE/X-LARGE)**

STITCH KEY

⬭ = chain (ch)

╳ = double crochet (dc)

┼ = treble crochet (tr)

⋔ = 3-tr cluster (3-tr CL)

⋔ = 5-tr cluster (5-tr CL)

⋔ = 7-tr cluster (7-tr CL)

⋯⋯ = camouflage (A)

─── = purple (B)

**PANEL 2
(SIZE SMALL/MEDIUM)
(WORK 1 MORE REP FOR LARGE/X-LARGE)**

marguerite jacket

OVERVIEW

Each hank of this yarn is unique with varying colour and thickness; to achieve overall blending and moiré effect, alternate one row of each of 3 balls and strand yarn up edges of piece without cutting when switching from one to the other—a decorative finish will be worked over the stranded yarn at front openings..

Jacket is worked in one piece from hem to armholes. There is no RS or WS to this stitch patt; before assembling decide which side of fabric has the better coloration and texture.

BODY

With first ball of yarn make 115 (123, 131, 139, 147, 155, 163, 171) ch. Work in M3C patt as given on page 98—56 (60, 64, 68, 72, 76, 80, 84) M3Cs. Join new ball of yarn and work patt Row 2. Join third ball of yarn and cont in M3C patt alternating among 3 balls, AT SAME TIME beg with next row shape sides as foll:

Shape Sides

Row 3: *Work 12 (13, 14, 15, 16, 17, 18, 19) M3Cs, dec 1 M3C over the next 2 M3Cs, work in patt across to within last 13 (14, 15, 16, 17, 18, 19, 20) M3Cs, dec 1 M3C over the next 2

Sized to fit snug (actual bust measurement) and very shaped; you can adjust for a less hour-glass shape by not working all the decreases at waist. **Shown in smallest size**	**MEASUREMENTS** Bust 83.8 (90.2, 95.9, 101.6, 107.3, 113, 118.7, 124.5) cm Length 52.1 (54.6, 55.9, 57.2, 58.4, 59.7, 61, 62.2) cm	**YARN** Mango Moon "Tone on Tone Viscose" (100% recycled rayon), worsted weight yarn 6 (7, 8, 9, 10, 11, 12, 13) hanks (3.5 oz/100 g; 150 yd/137 m) in mint	**HOOK** 5.5 mm (US I/9) or size needed to obtain gauge **NOTIONS** Tapestry needle 2 yards ribbon 6 mm to 1.3 cm wide (ribbon shown is gold lamé)	**GAUGE** 14 sts (7 M3Cs) and 8 rows = 10.2 cm in marguerite cluster pattern Always check and MATCH gauge for best results.

special stitches

MARGUERITE CLUSTER PATTERN (M3C patt)
Ch a multiple of 2 + 1 sts.

Note: Each Marguerite Cluster (M3C) is made up of a cluster and 1ch to secure cluster. Each M3C is counted as 1 st.

Row 1: Draw up a 1.9 cm loop in 2nd, 3rd, and 5th ch from hook, yo, draw yarn through 4 loops on hook (cluster made), 1ch to secure (first M3C made), *draw up a 1.9 cm loop in 1ch space (made to secure last M3C), draw up a 1.9 cm loop in base of last spike of last M3C, skip 1 ch, draw up a 1.9 cm loop in next ch, yo, draw yarn through 4 loops on hook, 1ch to secure (M3C made); rep from * across.

Row 2: 3ch, draw up a 1.9 cm loop in 2nd and 3rd ch from hook, skip first cluster, draw up a 1.9 cm loop next in 1ch space, yo, draw yarn through 4 loops on hook, 1ch to secure (first M3C made), *draw up a 1.9 cm loop in 1ch space made to secure last M3C, draw up a 1.9 cm loop in base of last spike of last M3C, skip next cluster, draw up a 1.9 cm loop in next 1ch space made to secure last M3C in previous row, yo, draw yarn through 4 loops on hook, 1ch to secure (M3C made); rep from * across, picking up final loop in 3rd ch of turning ch at end of previous row.

Rep Row 2 for patt.

Increasing in the middle of row: *Draw up a 1.9 cm oop in 1ch space made to secure last M3C, draw up a 1.9 cm loop in base of last spike of last M3C, do not skip next st, draw up a 1.9 cm loop in next cluster, yo, draw yarn through 4 loops on hook, 1ch to secure (M3C made), draw up a 1.9 cm loop in next 1ch space (made to secure last M3C); rep from * once (inc 1 M3C made).

Decreasing at beg of row: 3ch, draw up a 1.9 cm loop in 2nd and 3rd ch from hook, skip first cluster, draw up a loop in next 1ch space, skip next cluster, draw up a loop in next 1ch space, yo, draw yarn through 5 loops on hook, 1ch to secure (dec M3C made),

Decreasing in middle or end of row: Draw up a 1.9 cm loop in 1ch space made to secure last M3C, draw up a loop in base of last spike of last M3C, (skip next cluster, draw up a loop in next 1ch space) twice, yo, draw yarn through 5 loops on hook, 1ch to secure (dec M3C made).

STITCH KEY

◠ = chain (ch)

⅂ = Marguerite Cluster (M3C)

REDUCED SAMPLE OF M3C PATTERN

M3Cs, work in patt across (2 M3Cs decreased)—54 (58, 62, 66, 70, 74, 78, 82) M3Cs.

Rows 4–5: Work even in M3C patt.

Rows 6–11: Rep Rows 3–5 twice—50 (54, 58, 62, 66, 70, 74, 78) M3Cs at end of last row.

Rows 12–16: Work even on 50 (54, 58, 62, 66, 70, 74, 78) M3Cs.

Inc at each side next row as foll:

Row 17: *Work 12 (13, 14, 15, 16, 17, 18, 19) M3Cs, inc 1 M3C in next M3C, work in patt across to within last 13 (14, 15, 16, 17, 18, 19, 20) M3Cs, inc 1 M3C in next M3C, work in patt across (2 M3Cs increased)—52 (56, 60, 64, 68, 72, 76, 80) M3Cs.

Row 18: Work even in M3C patt.

Rows 19–24: Rep Rows 17–18 3 times—58 (62, 66, 70, 74, 78, 82, 86) M3Cs at end of last row.

Work even on 58 (62, 66, 70, 74, 78, 82, 86) M3Cs until piece measures 33 cm from beg.

FIRST FRONT
Divide and Shape Front Armhole as foll:

Next Row: Work 13 (14, 15, 16, 17, 18, 19, 20) M3Cs, dec 1 M3C over the next 2 M3Cs to shape armhole, turn, leaving rem sts unworked—14 (15, 16, 17, 18, 19, 20, 21) M3Cs.

Dec 1 M3C at armhole edge every row twice—12 (13, 14, 15, 16, 17, 18, 19) M3Cs at end of last row.

Work even on 12 (13, 14, 15, 16, 17, 18, 19) M3Cs until armhole measures 12.7 cm from beg.

Next Row: Inc 1 M3C at armhole edge—13 (14, 15, 16, 17, 18, 19, 20) M3Cs.

Work even on 13 (14, 15, 16, 17, 18, 19, 20) M3Cs until armhole measures 16.5 (17.8, 19.1, 20.3, 21.6, 22.9, 24.1, 25.4) cm from beg.

Shape Front Neck/Shoulder

If next row is a RS row, work the next 3 rows:

Next Row: Sl st over first 5 (5, 6, 6, 7, 7, 8, 8) M3Cs, 2ch, work in M3C patt across, turn—8 (9, 9, 10, 10, 11, 11, 12) M3Cs.

Next Row: Work in M3C patt across to last 2 M3Cs, dec 1 M3C over the next 2 M3Cs, turn.

Next Row: Work in M3C patt across first 3 (4, 4, 5, 5, 5, 6, 6) M3Cs. Fasten off.

Or, if next row is a WS row, work the next 3 rows:

Next Row: Work in M3C patt across first 8 (9, 9, 10, 10, 11, 11, 12) M3Cs, turn, leaving rem sts unworked.

Next Row: Dec 1 M3C over first 2 M3C's, work in M3C patt across, turn—7 (8, 8, 9, 9, 10, 10, 11) M3Cs.

Next Row: Sl st over first 4 (4, 4, 4, 4, 4, 4, 5) M3Cs, 2ch, work in M3C patt across next 3 (4, 4, 5, 5, 5, 6, 6) M3Cs. Fasten off.

BACK

Next Row: With appropriate side facing, join yarn at armhole in base of last st made in first row of First Front, 2ch, dec 1 M3C over first 2 M3Cs, work in M3C patt across next 24 (26, 28, 30, 32, 34, 36, 38) M3Cs, dec 1 M3C over next 2 M3Cs—26 (28, 30,

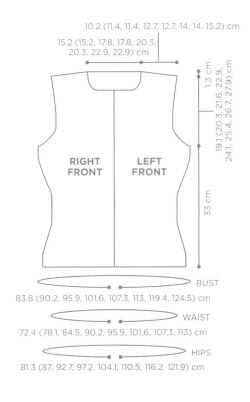

10.2 (11.4, 11.4, 12.7, 12.7, 14, 14, 15.2) cm

15.2 (15.2, 17.8, 17.8, 20.3, 20.3, 22.9, 22.9) cm

1.3 cm

19.1 (20.3, 21.6, 22.9, 24.1, 25.4, 26.7, 27.9) cm

RIGHT FRONT

LEFT FRONT

33 cm

BUST
83.8 (90.2, 95.9, 101.6, 107.3, 113, 119.4, 124.5) cm

WAIST
72.4 (78.1, 84.5, 90.2, 95.9, 101.6, 107.3, 113) cm

HIPS
81.3 (87, 92.7, 97.2, 104.1, 110.5, 116.2, 121.9) cm

33 (36.2, 39.4, 39.4, 41.9, 41.9, 45.1, 45.1) cm

12.7 (14, 14, 15.2, 15.2, 16.5, 16.5, 17.8) cm

25.4 cm

SLEEVE

27.9 (27.9, 30.5, 30.5, 33, 33, 36.2, 36.2) cm

32, 34, 36, 38, 40) M3Cs, turn, leaving rem sts unworked.

Shape Back Armholes

Work in M3C patt, dec 1 M3C at each end of every row twice—22 (24, 26, 28, 30, 32, 34, 36) M3Cs.

Work even on 22 (24, 26, 28, 30, 32, 34, 36) M3Cs until armhole measures 12.7 cm from beg.

Next Row: Inc 1 M3C at armhole edge—24 (26, 28, 30, 32, 34, 36, 38) M3Cs.

Work even on 24 (26, 28, 30, 32, 34, 36, 38) M3Cs until armhole measures 19.1 (20.3, 21.6, 22.9, 24.1, 25.4, 26.7, 27.9) cm from beg.

Shape Shoulders

Next Row: Sl st over first 4 (4, 4, 4, 4, 4, 4, 5), 2ch, work in M3C patt across to within last 4 (4, 4, 4, 4, 4, 4, 5) M3Cs, fasten off, leaving rem sts unworked—16 (18, 20, 22, 24, 26, 28, 28) M3Cs—[3 (4, 4, 5, 5, 5, 6, 6) each side for shoulders and 10 (10, 12, 12, 14, 14, 16, 16) M3Cs for centre neck.]

SECOND FRONT
Next Row: With appropriate side facing, join yarn at armhole in base of last st made in first row of Back, 2ch, dec 1 M3C over first 2 M3Cs, work in M3C patt across last 13 (14, 15, 16, 17, 18, 19, 20) M3Cs, turn—14 (15, 16, 17, 18, 19, 20, 21) M3Cs.

Work same as First Front, reversing shaping.

SLEEVE (make 2)
With first ball of yarn, make 41 (41, 45, 45, 49, 49, 53, 53) ch.

Work in M3C patt as est on 19 (19, 21, 21, 23, 23, 25, 25) M3Cs, alternating bet 3 balls of yarn as before, AT SAME TIME inc 1 M3C at beg and end of every 6th (4th, 4th, 4th, 4th, 4th, 4th, 4th) row 2 (3, 3, 3, 3, 3, 3, 3) times—23 (25, 27, 27, 29, 29, 31, 31) M3Cs at end of last row. Work even in M3C patt until Sleeve measures 25.4 cm from beg.

Shape Cap

Dec 1 M3C at beg and end of every row 6 times, work 0 (1, 1, 2, 2, 3, 3, 4) rows even, dec 1 M3C at beg and end of next row, work 1 row even, dec 1 M3C at beg and end of next 2 rows— 5 (7, 9, 9, 11, 11, 13, 13) M3Cs at end of last row, fasten off.

FINISHING
Sew shoulder and sleeve seams using tapestry needle. Set in sleeves, easing into armhole, and sew. Utilizing the yarn stranded every 3rd row along each edge, work as follows: slip st to lower right front edge, *5 dc over strand, dc into edge where this strand meets next; rep from * across. Fasten off at neck edge. Repeat for left front edge from neck to hem.

COLLAR
Join yarn at WS left neck edge, 3ch, skip 2.5 cm of neck edge, slip st into next st; rep from * turn around neck, work 4 dc in each 3ch loop across, dc in last slip st to end. Fasten off. Thread ribbon through holes in decorative trim from hem to collar to hem.

clover fan jacket

OVERVIEW

Jacket is worked from waist downward and then from waist upward so that pattern fans out from waist; sleeve is worked in similar manner by working cuff downward then working sleeve upward from cuff. Hourglass shaping is achieved by working more legs in fan motif. Because the pattern forms dramatic scallops, inserts are worked to level out fabric at top of pieces. Jacket is composed of 7 (7, 11) pattern reps; 3 (3, 5) across back and 2 (2, 3) across each front. Right Front is designed to overlap Left Front by approx 1 pattern rep.

HEM

With appropriate size hook for desired size, make 128 (128, 200) ch.

Foundation Row (WS): Dc in 2nd ch from the hook, *skip next 2 ch, 5 tr in next ch, skip next 2 ch, dc in next ch; rep from * across, turn—21 (21, 33) 5-tr shells made.

Rows 1–3: Work Rows 1–3 of Clover Fan Pattern I—7 (7, 11) pattern reps.

Row 4: To prepare for Clover Fan Pattern II, work Transition Row 4.

Rows 5–11: Working in Clover Fan Pattern II, work Rows 1–4, then rep Rows 1–3. Fasten off.

The width and placement of the motif on this garment makes providing multiple sizes in close range problematic. However, its wide wrap front allows for greater range of fit for each size.

Directions are given for women's size small (2–6). Changes for medium (8–12) and X-large (Women's sizes 20–3X)

are in parentheses. *(Note: Sizes small and medium are worked from the same instructions using a different size hook.)*

Shown in medium and large sizes

MEASUREMENTS

Bust: 87.6 (94, 147.3) cm with centre panels overlapped by approx. 11.4 (12.7, 17.8) cm

Waist: 68.6 (76.2, 114.3) cm
Length 50.8 (61, 69.9)cm

YARN

Blue Sky Alpacas "Blue Sky Cotton" (100% cotton), worsted weight yarn

10 (12, 15) hanks (3.5 oz/100 g; 150 yd/137 m), Size medium shown in #601 poppy; Size X-large shown in #625 graphite.

HOOK

For sizes small and X-large: 5.5 mm (US I/9) or size to match gauge.

For size medium: 6 mm (US J/10) or size to match gauge

GAUGE

For sizes small and X-large, with smaller hook, 18 ch at waist = 11.4 cm; In Clover Fan Pattern I, one pattern rep = 12.7 cm;

In Clover Fan Pattern II, one pattern rep = 16.5 cm; 4 rows in pattern = 6.4 cm

For size medium, with larger hook, 18 ch at waist = 12.7 cm; In Clover Fan Pattern I, one pattern rep = 14 cm; In Clover Fan Pattern II, one pattern rep = 17.8 cm; 4 rows in pattern = 7.6 cm

Always check and MATCH gauge for best results.

special stitches

SINGLE LEG CLOVER CLUSTER (SLC)

(Yo, insert hook, yo, draw up a 2.5 cm loop) twice in same st (5 loops on hook), yo, draw through all except last loop, yo, draw through rem 2 loops.

DOUBLE LEG CLOVER CLUSTER (DLC)

(Yo, insert hook, yo, draw up a 2.5 cm loop) twice in st indicated for first leg (5 loops on hook), (yo, insert hook, yo, draw up a 2.5 cm loop) twice in st indicated for second leg (9 loops on hook), yo, draw through all except last loop, yo, draw through rem 2 loops.

CLOVER FAN PATTERN I (multiple of 18 plus 1, plus 1 for t-ch)

Foundation Row (WS): Dc in 2nd ch from the hook, *skip next 2 ch, 5 tr in next ch, skip next 2 ch, dc in next ch; rep from * across, turn.

Row 1 (RS): 3ch (counts as tr), 2 tr in first st, *skip next 2 tr, dc in next tr, 1ch, skip next (2 tr, dc), SLC in next tr, (2ch, DLC, working first leg in same st as last st made and working 2nd leg in next tr) 4 times, 2ch, SLC in same st as last st made, 1ch, skip next (dc, 2 tr), dc in next tr, skip next 2 tr, 5 tr in next dc; rep from * across, ending with 3 tr in last dc, turn.

Row 2: 1ch, dc in first tr, *skip next (2 tr, dc and ch), SLC in next tr, (2ch, DLC, working first leg in same st as last st made, skip next 2ch space, work 2nd leg in next st) 5 times, 2ch, SLC in same st as last st made, skip next (ch, dc and 2 tr), dc in next tr; rep from * across, ending last rep with dc in top of t-ch, turn.

Row 3: 1ch, dc in first dc, dc in each st across, working 2 dc in each 2ch space across, turn.

Row 4: 1ch, dc in first dc, *skip next 3 dc, 5 tr in next dc, (skip next 2 dc, dc in next dc, skip next 2 dc, 5 tr in next dc) twice, skip 3 dc, dc in next dc; rep from * across, turn.

Rep Rows 1–4 for pattern.

CLOVER FAN PATTERN I

CLOVER FAN PATTERN II

(Pattern begins after Row 3 of Pattern I by working a transition row to establish additional stitches. To maintain numerical sequence, Pattern II will begin with Transition Row 4 of pattern.)

Transition Row 4 (WS) (replaces centre shell of each fan with a 7-tr shell): 1ch, dc in first dc, *skip next 3 dc, 5 tr in next dc, skip next 2 dc, dc in next dc, skip next 2 dc, 7 tr in next dc, skip next 2 dc, dc in next dc, skip next 2 dc, 5 tr in next dc, skip next 3 dc, dc in next dc; rep from * across, turn.

Row 1 (RS) (works 2 extra DLC across each fan): 3ch (counts as tr), 2 tr in first dc, *skip next 2 tr, dc in next tr, 1ch, skip next (2 tr, dc), SLC in next tr, (2ch, DLC, working first leg in same st as last st made and working 2nd leg in next tr) 6 times, 2ch, SLC in same st as last st made, 1ch, skip next (dc, 2 tr), dc in next tr, skip next 2 tr, 5 tr in next dc; rep from * across, ending with 3 tr in last dc, turn.

Row 2 (works 2 extra DLC across each fan): 1ch, dc in first tr, *skip next (2 tr, dc and ch), SLC in next tr, (2ch, DLC, working first leg in same st as last st made, skip next 2ch space, work 2nd leg in next st) 7 times, 2ch, SLC in same st as last st made, skip next (ch, dc and 2 tr), dc in next tr; rep from * across, ending last rep with dc in top of t-ch, turn.

Row 3: 1ch, dc in first dc, dc in each st across, working 2 dc in each 2ch space across, turn.

Row 4: 1ch, dc in first dc, *skip next 4 dc, 5 tr in next dc, skip next 3 dc, dc in next dc, skip next 3 dc, 7 tr in next dc, skip next 3 dc, dc in next dc, skip next 3 dc, 5 tr in next dc, skip next 4 dc, dc in next dc; rep from * across, turn.

Rep Rows 1–4 for pattern.

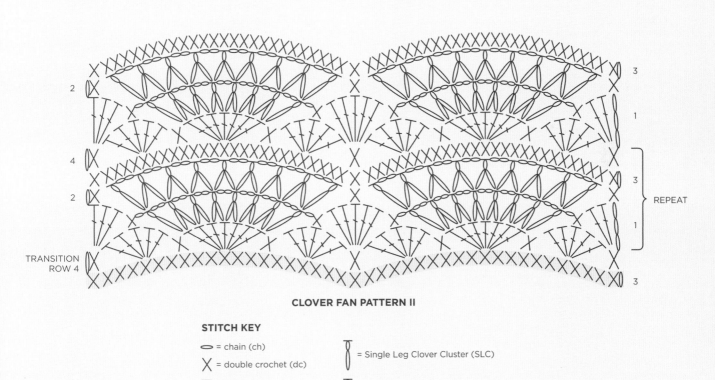

CLOVER FAN PATTERN II

STITCH KEY

⌒ = chain (ch)

X = double crochet (dc)

T = treble crochet (tr)

⏉ = Single Leg Clover Cluster (SLC)

⅄ = Double Leg Clover Cluster (DLC)

BODICE

Foundation Row (WS): *(Note: You can distinguish RS from WS by looking at Row 3 of pattern—after the 2 rows of clusters, Row 3 is all dc. On RS of fabric dc will have smooth top while on WS it will have bumpy top.)* With WS facing, using appropriate size hook for desired size, working across opposite side of foundation ch, join yarn in first ch, 1ch, dc in first ch, *skip next 2 ch, 5 tr in next ch, skip next 2 ch, dc in next ch; rep from * across, turn—21 (21, 33) 5-tr shells made.

Rows 1–7: Work in Clover Fan Pattern I, working Rows 1–4, then rep Rows 1–3.

Row 8: Work Transition Row 4 of Clover Fan Pattern II.

Sizes Small and Medium Only:
Rows 9–11: Working in Clover Fan Pattern II, work Rows 1–3.

Size X-Large Only: Rows 9–15: Working in Clover Fan Pattern II, work Rows 1–4, then rep Rows 1–3.

Sizes Small and Medium Only

LEFT FRONT

Row 12 (WS): 1ch, dc in first dc, *skip next 4 dc, 5 tr in next dc, skip next 3 dc, dc in next dc, skip next 3 dc, 7 tr in next dc, skip next 3 dc, dc in next dc, skip next 3 dc, 5 tr in next dc, skip next 4 dc, dc in next dc; rep from * once, turn, leaving rem sts unworked.

Rows 13–19: Working in Clover Fan Pattern II, work Rows 1–4, then rep Rows 1–3. Fasten off.

LEFT SHOULDER INSERT

Row 20: With WS facing, using appropriate size hook for desired size, skip first 26 dc, join yarn in next dc, 1ch, dc in same dc, *skip next 2 dc, 5 tr in next dc (aligns with DLC 2 rows below), skip next 2 dc, dc in next dc; rep from * once, turn.

Row 21: Sl st to centre tr of first shell, 1ch, dc in same st, skip next 2 tr, 5 tr in next tr, skip next 2 tr, dc in next tr, skip next 2 tr, 5 tr in next dc, turn.

Row 22: 3ch (count as first SLC), (2ch, DLC, working first leg in same st as last st made, work 2nd leg in next st) 4 times, 2ch, SLC in same st as last st made, skip next 2 tr, dc in each of next 3 tr. Fasten off.

BACK

Row 12: With WS facing, join yarn in same dc holding last dc in Row 12 of Left Front, 1ch, dc in first dc, *skip next 4 dc, 5 tr in next dc, skip next 3 dc, dc in next dc, skip next 3 dc, 7 tr in next dc, skip next 3 dc, dc in next dc, skip next 3 dc, 5 tr in next dc, skip next 4 dc, dc in next dc; rep from * twice, turn.

Rows 13–19: Working in Clover Fan Pattern II, work Rows 1–4, then rep Rows 1–3 on 3 reps. Fasten off.

BACK LEFT SHOULDER INSERT

Row 20: With WS facing, skip first 13 dc, join yarn in next dc, 1ch, dc in same dc, skip next 2 dc, *5 tr in next dc, skip next 2 dc, dc in next dc, skip next 2 dc, 5 tr in next dc, *skip next 3 dc, dc in next dc, *skip next 3 dc, rep, skip next 2 dc, dc in next dc (centre dc of Back), turn, leaving rem sts unworked.

Row 21: Sl st to centre tr of first shell, 1ch, dc in same st, *skip next 2 tr, 5 tr in next dc, skip next 2 tr, dc in next tr; rep from * twice, turn, leaving rem sts unworked.

Row 22: 1ch, skip first dc, dc in each of next 3 tr, skip next (2 tr and dc), SLC in next tr, (2ch, DLC, working first leg in same st as last st made, work 2nd leg in next st) 4 times, 2ch, SLC in same st as last st made, skip next dc and 2 tr, dc in each of next 3 tr. Fasten off.

BACK RIGHT SHOULDER INSERT

Row 20: With WS facing, join yarn in centre dc of Back (last st in Row 20 of Back Left Shoulder Insert), 1ch, dc in same dc, skip next 2 dc, 5 tr in next dc, skip next 2 dc, dc in next dc, skip next 2 dc, 5 tr in next dc, *skip

next 3 dc, dc in next dc, skip next 3 dc, rep between * and *, skip next 2 dc, dc in next dc (centre dc of row), turn, leaving rem sts unworked.

Rows 21–22: Rep Rows 21–22 of Back Left Shoulder Insert. Fasten off.

RIGHT FRONT

Row 12: With WS facing, join yarn in same dc holding last dc in Row 12 of Back, 1ch, dc in first dc, *skip next 4 dc, 5 tr in next dc, skip next 3 dc, dc in next dc, skip next 3 dc, 7 tr in next dc, skip next 3 dc, dc in next dc, skip next 3 dc, 5 tr in next dc, skip next 4 dc, dc in next dc; rep from * once, turn.

Rows 13–19: Working in Clover Fan Pattern II, work Rows 1–4, then rep Rows 1–3 on 2 reps. Fasten off.

RIGHT SHOULDER INSERT

Row 20: With WS facing. using appropriate size hook for desired size, skip first 13 dc, join yarn in next dc (centre dc over first fan), 1ch, dc in same dc, *skip next 2 dc, 5 tr in next dc (aligns with DLC 2 rows below), skip next 2 dc, dc in next dc; rep from * once, turn.

Row 21: 3ch (counts as tr), 4 tr in first dc, skip next 2 tr, dc in next tr, skip next 2 tr, 5 tr in next dc, skip next 2 tr, dc in next tr, turn, leaving rem sts unworked.

Row 22: 1ch, skip first dc, dc in each of next 3 tr, skip next 2 tr, SLC in next dc, (2ch, DLC, working first leg in same st as last st made, work 2nd leg in next st) 5 times, ending with last leg in top of t-ch. Fasten off.

Size Large

LEFT FRONT

Row 12 (WS): 1ch, dc in first dc, *skip next 4 dc, 5 tr in next dc, skip next 3 dc, dc in next dc, skip next 3 dc, 7 tr in next dc, skip next 3 dc, dc in next dc, skip next 3 dc, 5 tr in next dc, skip next 4 dc, dc in next dc; rep from * once, skip next 4 dc, 5 tr in next dc, skip next 3 dc, dc in next dc, skip next 3 dc, 4 tr in next dc, turn, leaving rem sts unworked—2 ½ reps.

Row 13: 3ch (counts as SLC), (2ch, DLC, working first leg in same st as last st made and working 2nd leg in next tr) 3 times, 2ch, SLC in same st as last st made, 1ch, skip next (dc, 2 tr), work in est pattern of Clover Fan Pattern II Row 1 across, turn—2 ½ reps.

Row 14: Work in Clover Fan Pattern II Row 2 across first 2 reps, ending with skip next (2 tr, dc and ch), SLC in next tr, (2ch, DLC, working first leg in same st as last st made, skip next

2ch space, work 2nd leg in next st) 4 times, ending with last leg of last DLC in top of t-ch, turn—2 ½ reps.

Row 15: 1ch, dc in first dc, dc in each st across, working 2 dc in each 2ch space across, turn—2 ½ reps.

Rows 16–23: Rep last 4 rows twice.

LEFT SHOULDER INSERT
Row 24: With WS facing, skip first 39 dc, join yarn in next dc, 1ch, dc in same dc, skip next 2 dc, 5 tr in next dc, skip next 3 dc, dc in next dc, skip next 3 dc, 5 tr in next dc, skip next 2 dc, dc in next dc, skip next 2 dc, 5 tr

in next dc, skip next 2 dc, dc in next dc, turn, leaving rem sts unworked.

Row 25: Sl st to centre tr of first shell, 1ch, dc in same st, *skip next 2 tr, 5 tr in next dc, skip next 2 tr, dc in next tr; rep from * twice, turn, leaving rem sts unworked.

Row 26: 1ch, skip first dc, dc in each of next 3 tr, skip next (2 tr and dc), SLC in next tr, (2ch, DLC, working first leg in same st as last st made, skip next 2ch space, work 2nd leg in next st) 4 times, 2ch, SLC in same st as last st made, skip next 2 tr, dc in each of next 3 tr. Fasten off.

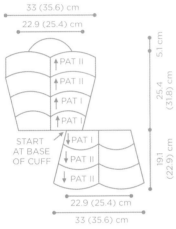

SIZE SMALL AND MEDIUM SLEEVE

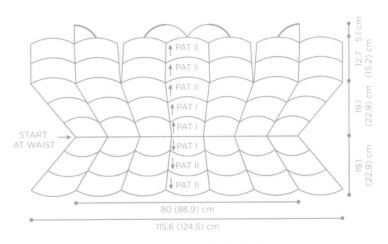

SIZES SMALL AND MEDIUM BODY

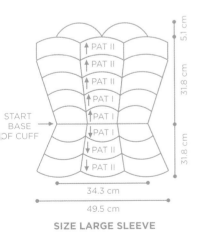

SIZE LARGE SLEEVE

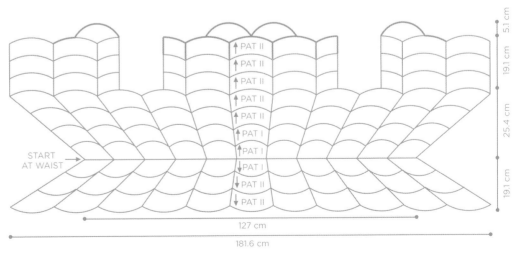

SIZE LARGE BODY

BACK

Row 12: With WS facing, skip 25 dc to the left of last st made in Row 12 of Left Front, 3ch (counts as tr), 4 tr in first dc, skip next 3 dc, dc in next dc, skip next 3 dc, 5 tr in next dc, skip next 4 dc, dc in next dc, *skip next 4 dc, 5 tr in next dc, skip next 3 dc, dc in next dc, skip next 3 dc, 7 tr in next dc, skip next 3 dc, dc in next dc, skip next 3 dc, 5 tr in next dc, skip next 4 dc, dc in next dc; rep from * twice, skip next 4 dc, 5 tr in next dc, skip next 3 dc, dc in next dc, skip next 3 dc, 4 tr in last dc, turn—3 full reps and one half rep on each end.

Row 13: 3ch (counts as SLC), (DLC, working first leg in same st as last st made and working 2nd leg in next tr, 2ch) 3 times, SLC in same st as last st made, 1ch, work in est pattern of Clover Fan Pattern II Row 1 across 3 reps, ending with 5 tr in next dc, skip next 2 tr, dc in next dc, skip next (2 tr, and dc), SLC in next tr, (2ch, DLC, working first leg in same st as last st made and working 2nd leg in next tr) 3 times, SLC in top of t-ch already holding last st, turn—3 full reps and one half rep on each end.

Row 14: 3ch, skip first st, SLC in next st, (2ch, DLC, working first leg in same st as last st made and working 2nd leg in next tr) 3 times, 2ch, SLC in same st as last st made, work in est pattern of Clover Fan Pattern II Row 2 across 3 reps, ending with skip next (2 tr, dc and ch), SLC in next tr, (2ch, DLC, working first leg in same st as last st made, skip next 2ch space, work 2nd leg in next st) 4 times, ending with last leg of last DLC in top of t-ch, turn—3 full reps and one half rep on each end.

Row 15: 1ch, dc in first dc, dc in each st across, working 2 dc in each 2ch space across, turn.

Rows 16–23: Rep last 4 rows twice.

BACK LEFT SHOULDER INSERT

With WS facing, skip first 26 dc, join yarn in next dc, work Rows 24–26 of Left Shoulder Insert.

BACK RIGHT SHOULDER INSERT

With WS facing, join yarn in same dc holding last dc in first row of Back Left Shoulder Insert, work Rows 24–26 of Left Shoulder Insert.

RIGHT FRONT

Row 12: With WS facing, skip 25 dc to the left of last st made in Row 12 of Back, 3ch (counts as tr), 4 tr in first dc, skip next 3 dc, dc in next dc, skip next 3 dc, 5 tr in next dc, skip next 4 dc, dc in next dc, work in est pattern of Clover Fan Pattern II Row 4 across 2 reps, turn—2 ½ reps.

Row 13: 3ch (counts as tr), 2 tr in first st, *skip next 2 tr, dc in next tr, 1ch, skip next (2 tr, dc), SLC in next tr, (2ch, DLC, working first leg in same st as last st made and working 2nd leg in next tr) 6 times, 2ch, SLC in same st as last st made, 1ch, skip next (dc, 2 tr), dc in next tr, skip next 2 tr, 5 tr in next dc; rep from * once, ending with skip next 2 tr, dc in next dc, skip next (2 tr, and dc), SLC in next tr, (2ch, DLC, working first leg in same st as last st made and working 2nd leg in next tr) 3 times, 2ch, SLC in top of t-ch already holding last st, turn—2 ½ reps.

Row 14: 3ch, skip first st, SLC in next st, (2ch, DLC, working first leg in same st as last st made and working 2nd leg in next tr) 3 times, 2ch, SLC

in same st as last st made, work in est pattern of Clover Fan Pattern II Row 2 across 2 reps, turn—2 1/2 reps.

Row 15: 1ch, dc in first dc, dc in each st across, working 2 dc in each 2ch spaces across, turn.

Rows 16–23: Rep last 4 rows twice. Do not fasten off.

RIGHT SHOULDER INSERT

Starting in first st, work Rows 24–26 of Left Shoulder Insert.

All Sizes

SLEEVE (make 2)

Cuff: With appropriate size hook for desired size, ch 38 (38, 56).

Foundation Row (WS): Dc in 2nd ch from the hook, *skip next 2 ch, 5 tr in next ch, skip next 2 ch, dc in next ch; rep from * across, turn—6 (6, 9) 5-tr shells made.

Rows 1–3: Work Rows 1–3 of Clover Fan Pattern I—2 (2, 3) pattern reps.

Row 4: To prepare for Clover Fan Pattern II, work Transition Row 4.

Rows 5–11: Working in Clover Fan Pattern II, work Rows 1–4, then rep Rows 1–3. Fasten off.

Sizes Small and Medium Only

UPPER SLEEVE

Sew cuff seam. You will start the Upper Sleeve beg one half stitch pattern in from edge so that fan on cuff is centered over hand.

Foundation Row: With WS facing, working across opposite side of foundation ch, skip first 10 ch, join yarn in next ch (at base of 2nd shell), 1ch, dc in same ch, *skip next 2 ch, 5 tr in next ch, skip next 2 ch, dc in next ch; rep from * across to seam, then continue to work across other side of Cuff foundation ch to beg, turn—6 (6) 5-tr shells made.

Rows 1–7: Work in Clover Fan Pattern I, working Rows 1–4, then rep Rows 1–3.

Row 8: Work Transition Row 4 of Clover Fan Pattern II.

Rows 9–15: Working in Clover Fan Pattern II, work Rows 1–4, then rep Rows 1–3. Fasten off.

SLEEVE INSERT

(for Sleeve Cap)
With WS facing, skip first 13 dc, join yarn in next dc, work as for sizes Small/Medium Back Left Shoulder Insert. Fasten off.

Size Large Only

UPPER SLEEVE

Sew cuff seam.

Foundation Row: With WS facing, working across opposite side of foundation ch, join yarn in first ch, 1ch, dc in same ch, *skip next 2 ch, 5 tr in next ch, skip next 2 ch, dc in next ch; rep from * across, turn—9 5-tr shells made.

Rows 1–7: Work in Clover Fan Pattern I, working Rows 1–4, then rep Rows 1–3.

Row 8: Work Transition Row 4 of Clover Fan Pattern II.

Rows 9–19: Working in Clover Fan Pattern II, work Rows 1–4 (twice), then rep Rows 1–3. Fasten off.

SLEEVE INSERT

(for Sleeve Cap)
With WS facing, skip first 13 dc, join yarn in next dc, work as for size Large Left Shoulder Insert.

Rep size Large Right Shoulder Insert. Fasten off.

All Sizes

FINISHING

Sew shoulder seams. Sew sleeve seams, and ease sleeve cap (from base of last pattern rep and up through insertion) in armhole (for sizes Small and Medium armhole is from base of second to last pattern rep along to centre top of last pattern rep where insertion begins) and attach with dc on WS.

COLLAR

With appropriate size hook for desired size, make 56 (56, 74) ch.

Foundation Row (WS): Dc in 2nd ch from the hook, *skip next 2 ch, 5 tr in next ch, skip next 2 ch, dc in next ch; rep from * across, turn—3 (3, 4) 5-tr shells made.

Rows 1–3: Work Rows 1–3 of Clover Fan Pattern I—3 (3, 4) pattern reps.

Row 4: To prepare for Clover Fan Pattern II, work Transition Row 4.

Rows 5–7: Working in Clover Fan Pattern II, work Rows 1–3. Do not fasten off.

SIDE EDGING

Dc evenly down side edge of Collar. Fasten off. With WS facing, join yarn at base of first row of Collar on other side edge, dc evenly across. Fasten off.

ASSEMBLY

With RS of Collar and WS of Body tog, align centre of foundation ch of Collar with centre back neck of jacket, with ends of Collar meeting base of Front Inserts. Working through double thickness, join yarn in first st at base of Collar, 1ch, dc evenly across joining Collar to body. *(Note: When Collar is folded down, RS will be facing.)* Sew 3 dc along Collar side edge to corresponding 3 dc from last row at front neck opening to form notched collar. Rep on other side of Collar.

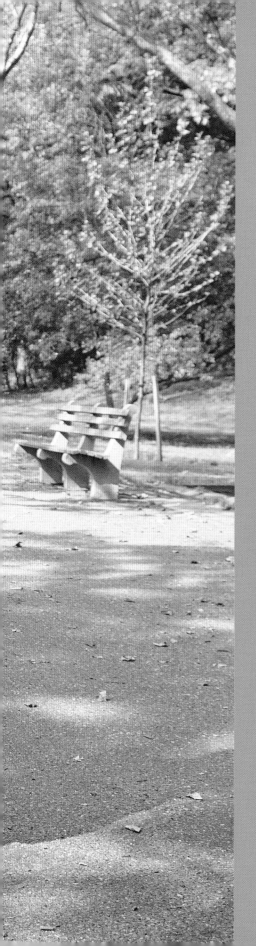

CHAPTER 5

Semi-Irish, Freeform-ish, and Granny-Style Crochet

SEMI-IRISH, FREEFORM-ISH, AND GRANNY-STYLE CROCHET

IN THIS FINAL CHAPTER, I PRESENT SEVERAL TYPES OF PIECED CROCHET—each is my own peculiar twist on the original. Irish crochet developed as a cottage industry to imitate elaborate Renaissance lace and relied on crocheting motifs, basting them onto muslin templates and then improvising various fillers of netting between them. In true Irish crochet the motifs are worked over cord to stand out in relief and several weights of thread are used. My "semi-Irish" crochet is a simplified version, yet looks quite organic and jumbled, revealing its connection to freeform crochet.

In freeform crochet, which started in the 1960s, "scrumbled" improvisational motifs are built upon each other to create an abstract composition. The idea is to play with the juxtaposition of colour and texture and follow the piece wherever it takes you. Most freeformers believe instructions are contrary to this notion. Once a pattern is given, it's called freeform-ish.

Granny squares—those colorful, patchwork yarn mosaics—are ubiquitous to crochet. I have omitted any standard granny-square fare here, but their quiltlike style does have some impact, as does my own granny. Certainly, if my fashions are ever "over the top," it is due to her influence. Disinherited for eloping with and then divorcing a communist poet, she made much of her own couture-quality wardrobe. She was obsessed with her lost social status and became progressively manic and paranoid. When I was in junior high, she'd visit daily, loaded down with bags of knitting projects and tabloids. As she stitched, we'd browse the celebrity gossip together—though not exactly on the same wavelength. She would talk incessantly—the Pope was sending her messages through Liz Taylor's reported moves, and I was supposed to marry JFK, Jr., but a spy conspiracy was spoiling her plans because I didn't have a proper trousseau. In need of meds as she was, Nani convinced me I could design and sew my own prom dress, and she bought me $75 a metre, hand-embroidered fabric—only the best would do if I was to catch a Kennedy. And so I executed my first design, a flouncy off-the-shoulder dress of gathered tiers.

Years later, it's that unconventional spirit I've brought to the designs in this chapter. While each is based on a traditional crochet technique, the result is something of my own.

star sphere purse and toy

Crocheted circles are everywhere, embellishing T-shirts and shoes and strung into belts. Working this star motif is a cinch in crochet, not much more difficult than making a plain circle. I was attracted to the star pattern for its folksy Americana quality; it resembles a patchwork quilt motif. Arranging a triad of points makes an intriguing composition, but it also creates a fabric that is convex rather than flat, so I've sewn these motifs into spheres that can serve as either a purse, pillow, or toddler toy. The edges of the motifs are quilted together with simple but decorative running stitch, making the motif-joining a nice project for an older sibling if the project is destined to be a baby toy. Younger kids enjoy helping with the stuffing.

>> See pattern on page 118.

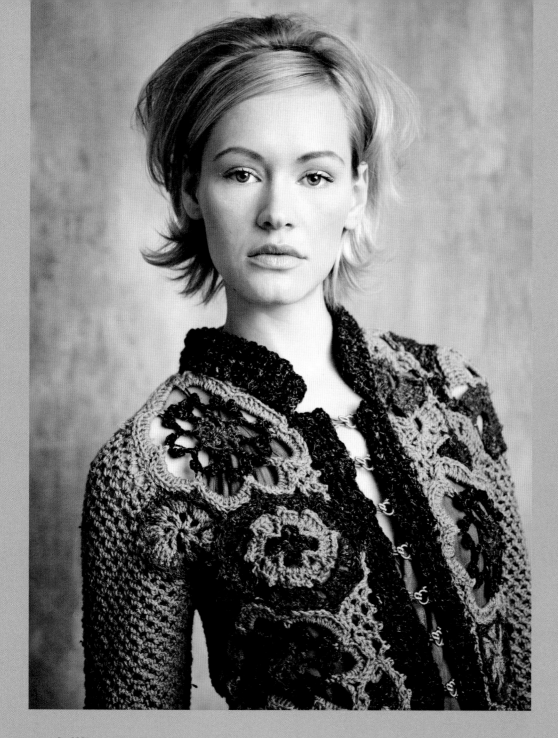

medallion cardigan and hat

This set is another venture into semi-Irish, freeformish crochet. The cardigan's back and sleeves are a simple net pattern, but the front is a composition of various whorls with net fill-ins. The ribbing is done by alternately crocheting around the front and back of work to imitate knitted ribbing. I selected a tweedy yarn for its retro feel and because the multiple flecks of colour and wiry white viscose hairs that run throughout integrate the components. Large fabric-covered hooks and eyes and a fanned Mandarin collar lend an Oriental appeal.

Instead of making a gauge swatch for the cardigan, you can simply start with the hat. I plan to make several as gifts using various spare medallions (I overshot my estimate of how many would fill the cardigan's fronts).

>> See pattern on page 122.

solomon knot flower shawl

This shawl is reminiscent of Irish crochet, but on a giant scale in bulky yarns. The combination of matte and shiny yarns gives the flowers sculptural depth. Rather than using a chain stitch for the net, which would double the yarn on itself and be stiff, I've used a knotted crochet technique that shows off the individual strands of yarn. The technique is named Solomon's Knot, which is the name of a similar motif in Celtic scrollwork that illuminated manuscripts in the Middle Ages, when it was believed that wearing an amulet of Solomon's Knot could ward off fevers.

>> See pattern on page 130.

lazy wheels coat

I consider this last piece in the collection to be the "wedding dress" —the customary finale to a runway show. Its train is created by sewing together motifs known as Lazy Wheel spirals in an interlocking formation. I love the Lazy Wheel pattern because it is like one of my favorite knitting techniques— creating a spiraling circle from the radius around. But in crochet, the wedgelike segments of the circle are much more easily made with shorter to longer stitches.

The textural ridges that highlight each segment and trim the coat are done by crocheting in a reverse direction. For the body of the coat, I adjusted a standard chevron pattern so that it undulates at an uneven rate—I wanted the arabesques and dips of Art Nouveau instead of a regulated zigzag. The buckles are a modern touch.

>> See pattern on page 134.

star sphere purse and toy

OVERVIEW

This sphere is pieced from 12 star motifs; the motifs are seamed with decorative stitch from star point to star point with seams folded outward like a quilt composed of pentagon motifs.

When working this two-colour motif the colour not in use is stranded loosely across back of work. Be sure to work first st of each round as this will give rounded star in which each leg comes to central point—if you skip the first st the motif shifts and forms a pinwheel.

STAR (make 6 with A for background and B for CC; make 6 with A for background and C for CC) With CC, make 4ch, join with sl st in first ch.

Rnd 1: With CC, 3ch (counts as tr), 14 tr in ring, sl st in top of t-ch—15 sts.

Rnd 2: With CC, 3ch (counts as tr), tr in first st, 2 tr in each tr around, sl st in top of t-ch—30 sts.

Rnd 3: With CC, 3ch (counts as tr), *with CC, tr in next st, tr2tog over next 2 sts, tr in each of next 2 sts, change to A, with A, 2 tr in same place as last tr, 2 tr in next st, change to CC**, with CC, tr in same place as

MEASUREMENTS	YARN	HOOK	For purse:	GAUGE
Each star motif is 12.1 cm in diameter	Mostly Merino "Light Sport/Fingering Fine Vermont Wool" (77% merino & corriedale wool/23% mohair), light sport weight yarn	1.9 mm (US steel 5) or size to match gauge	0.5 m lining fabric (I used vintage reproduction cotton "steamer trunk treasures" from Purl Patchwork, see Resources)	1 star motif = 12.1 cm in diameter
Sewn together and stuffed, sphere measures 61 cm in circumference	1 hank (2 oz/57 g; 250 yd/229 m) in monkshood (violet blue) (A);	**NOTIONS** Tapestry needle **For pillow:** Fiberfill Jingle bell (optional)	Wooden Handle Dritz 9809	Always check and MATCH gauge for best results.
	1 hank in tansy (yellow) (B);		Wooden bead	
	1 hank in raspberry (C)			

last tr; rep from * around, ending last rep at **, sl st in top of t-ch—45 sts.

Rnd 4: With CC, 3ch (counts as tr), *with CC, tr2tog over next 2 sts, tr in each of next 2 sts, change to A, with A, 2 tr in next st, tr in each of next 2 sts, 2 tr in next st, change to CC**, with CC, tr in next st; rep from * around, ending last rep at **, sl st in top of t-ch—50 sts.

Rnd 5: With CC, 3ch (counts as tr), *with CC, tr2tog over next 2 sts, tr in next st, change to A, with A, 2 tr in next st, tr in next st, 2 tr in each of next 2 sts, tr in next st, 2 tr in next st, change to CC**, with CC, tr in next st; rep from * around, ending last rep at **, sl st in top of t-ch—65 sts.

Rnd 6: With CC, 3ch (counts as tr), *with CC, tr2tog over next 2 sts, change to A, with A, 3 tr in next st, (tr in each of next 2 sts, 2 tr in next st) twice, tr in each of next 2 sts, 3 tr in next st, change to CC**, tr3tog over next 3 sts; rep from * around, ending last rep at **, sl st in top of t-ch—85 sts.

ASSEMBLY

Form First Half Sphere (see Assembly Diagram): Sew 6 motifs as foll: Arrange five B star motifs around one C star motif with star points touching (three star points of three different motifs should be touching at every intersection). Thread tapestry needle with B. With WS of star motifs together, RS facing, seam with running stitch 6mm in from edge on RS of fabric, letting seams fall to outside of work as decorative ridge.

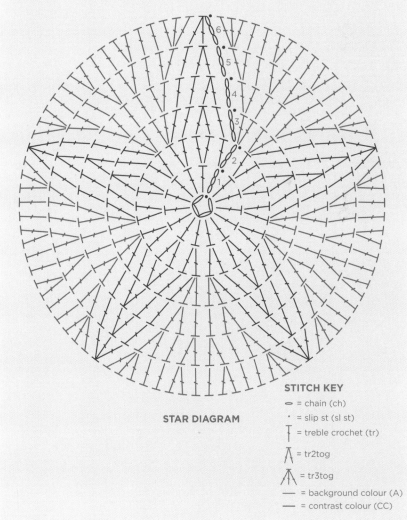

STAR DIAGRAM

STITCH KEY
⌒ = chain (ch)
• = slip st (sl st)
T = treble crochet (tr)
Λ = tr2tog
⋀ = tr3tog
— = background colour (A)
— = contrast colour (CC)

FOR TOY

Make Second Half Sphere of five C star motifs around one B star motif. Fit the two half spheres together and sew sides in same manner (three star points of three different motifs should be touching at every intersection). When opening is still wide enough (with 3 seams left to sew) stuff with fiberfill (and bells if desired).

FOR PURSE

For Second Half Sphere, fit five C star motifs around the First Half Sphere, arranged again so that three star points of three different motifs are touching at every intersection. Sew sides in same manner. Sew final B star motif at two sides only, leaving 3 sides open for purse flap. Work running stitch with B, 6 mm in from edge around all unseamed edges. Sew bead to centre front motif opposite centre of purse flap 1.3 cm in from edge. Make a ring at centre

front of purse flap as follows: With tapestry needle and B, sew 4 loops long enough to accommodate bead. Cut yarn, leaving a 3-metre tail. With end, work dc over all 4 loops until covered. Fasten off.

PURSE LINING

Trace around one motif adding 6 mm seam allowance all around and cut fabric to size. Sew to WS of purse flap motif (aligning grain of fabric to front of flap) with seam allowances of fabric folded under. Cut a wide circle of fabric approximately 38.1 cm in diameter adding 1.6 cm seam allowance. Baste around circumference of circle just inside seam allowance with long running stitch and pull thread to gather fabric until circumference approximates size of purse opening. Place in purse with RS of fabric facing outward and turning seam allowance under, sew to top of opening following the scalloped edge created by the joined motifs.

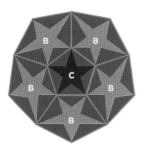

FIRST HALF SPHERE

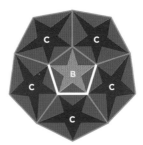

SECOND HALF SPHERE

ASSEMBLY DIAGRAM

medallion cardigan and hat

The Cardigan Waistband and Front Bands are made in Mock Rib stitch in one piece. Back and Sleeves are worked in Mesh Stitch. Using Back as a "template," Medallions are arranged for Fronts, sewn together with needle and thread where edges meet, and surrounding spaces are filled in with mesh st. For sewing, use whip stitch from RS, but bend pieces so WS pieces are pressed together and stitching will not show from RS.

MEDALLIONS See diagrams on page 124–25.

AMANDA WHORL (AW—make 1) 8 segments are worked with each segment done in successive colour: B, C, D, E, B, C, D, E

Segment 1

Foundation: With B, make 13ch, join with sl st to form base ring.

Row 1 (RS): 4ch (counts as dtr), (dtr in ring, 6ch, tr in top of dtr just made, dtr in ring) 3 times, dtr in ring, 2ch, 10 dtr in ring, turn.

Row 2: 5ch, sl st in 5th ch from hook to form Picot, skip first dtr, dc in each of next 9 dtr, change to C, turn.

Segment 2

Foundation: 1ch, dc in first dc, 3ch, skip next 3 dc, dc in next dc, 9ch, turn, skip next 3ch loop, sl st in first dc to complete joined base ring.

Row 1: Rep Row 1 of Segment 1

Row 2: 2ch, dc in 5ch Picot of previous Segment, 3ch, sl st in first ch of

MEASUREMENTS

Bust: 81.3 (90.8, 99.7, 108.6) cm closed including 2.5 cm at front opening for hooks and eyes

Waist: 68.6 (74.9, 81.3, 87.6) cm closed including 2.5 cm at front opening for hooks and eyes

Length: 57.2 (58.4, 59.7, 61) cm

Shown in smallest size.

Hat sized for child (adult): 40 (47) cm in circumference unstretched

YARN

Needful Yarns "Everest" (95% wool /5% viscose), worsted weight tweed

For Cardigan: 4 (4, 5, 5) balls (1.75 oz/50 g; 109 yd/100 m) in #6970 burgundy (A); 6 (6, 7, 8) balls in #6961 taupe (B); 2 balls

each in #6968 navy (C), #6962 light blue (D), and #6969 teal (E)

For Hat: 1 ball in #6962 light blue (D); small amounts C (or other colour for rib) and small amounts of A, B, and E to make 1 Briar Rose Medallion

HOOKS

3.5 mm (US E/3) or size to match gauge

NOTIONS

Sewing needle and strong thread to match B

11 covered hooks and eyes 1.6 cm wide to match B

GAUGE

20 sts and 12 rows = 10.2 cm in mock rib stitch pattern unstretched

5 3ch loops and 10 rows = 7.6 cm in mesh stitch pattern

Always check and MATCH gauge for best results—Make Hat (instructions begin on page 126) for Gauge Swatch.

row to complete Picot, skip first dtr, dc in each of next 9 dtr, change to next colour, turn.

Work 5 more segments as for Segment 2 in colour sequence.

Segment 8

With E, work same as Segment 2 through Row 1, then join to Segment 7 and Segment 1 as foll:

Row 2: 2ch, dc in Picot of Segment 7, 1ch, dc in Picot of Segment 1, 2ch, sl st in first ch of row to complete picot, skip first dtr, dc in each of next 5 dtr, sl st to Segment 1 at bottom of base ring, dc in each of next 4 dtr, sl st to Segment 1 at top of base ring. Fasten off.

Centre Ring

With A, 6ch, join with sl st to form ring.

Rnd 1: 1ch, 11 dc in ring. Fasten off.

Place Centre Ring in middle of Amanda Whorl so that the decorative Picots border it. Use needle and thread to sew it in place with whip st.

CELTIC MOTIF (CM—make 2, plus make another through Rnd 2)
With A, make 6ch, join with sl st to form ring.

Rnd 1: (3ch, 2 tr in ring, 3ch, sl st in ring) 4 times in ring—4 Spokes made. Fasten off.

Rnd 2: Join D in same place, 6ch (counts as tr, 3ch), skip next Spoke, *(tr, 3ch, tr) in next sl st, 3ch, skip next Spoke; rep from * twice more, tr in next sl st, 3ch, sl st to 3rd ch of 6ch to join—8 3ch loops made.

Rnd 3: 1ch, dc in same place as sl st, *3ch, 3 tr, in next 3ch loop, 3ch**, dc in next tr; rep from * around, ending last rep at **, sl st in first dc to join—8 Spokes made. Fasten off.

Rnd 4: Join C in same place, 1ch, dc in same place as sl st, *4ch, skip next Spoke, dc in next dc; rep from * around, omitting last dc, sl st to first dc to join—8 4ch loops made.

REDUCED SAMPLE OF MESH PATTERN

REDUCED SAMPLE OF MOCK RIB STITCH

STITCH KEY

- ⌒ = chain (ch)
- • = slip st (sl st)
- X = double crochet (dc)
- T = half treble crochet (htr)
- ꓕ = treble crochet (tr)
- ꝰ = Front post treble crochet (FPtr)
- ꝯ = Back post treble crochet (BPtr)
- ꓕ = double treble crochet (dtr)

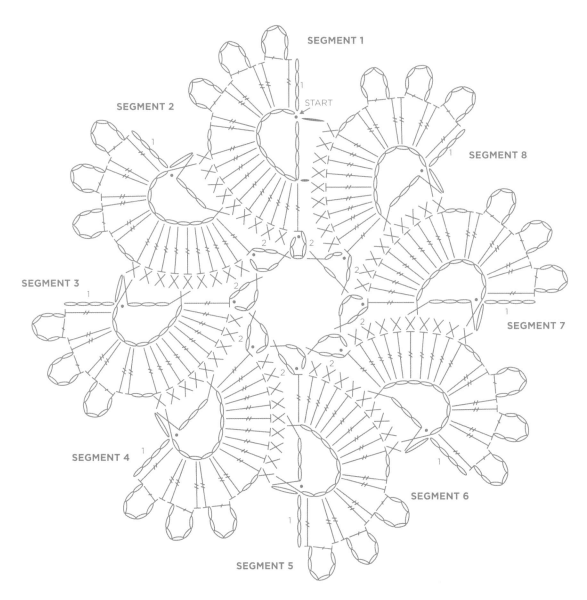

SEGMENT 1

SEGMENT 2

START

SEGMENT 8

SEGMENT 3

SEGMENT 7

SEGMENT 4

SEGMENT 6

SEGMENT 5

AMANDA WHORL MEDALLION

Rnd 5: 3ch (counts as tr), 4 tr in next 4ch loop, (2ch, 5 tr) in each 4ch loop around, 2ch, sl st to top of t-ch to join—8 2ch spaces made.

Rnd 6: 1ch, dc in same place as sl st, dc in each of next 4 tr, *(dc, 3ch, insert hook down through top of dc just made and work sl st to close for picot, dc) in next 2ch space**, dc in each of next 5 tr; rep from * around, ending last rep at **, sl st to first dc to join—8 picots made. Fasten off.

BRIAR ROSE (BR—make 3 for Cardigan, plus make 1 for Hat)
With E, 3ch, join with sl st to form ring.

Rnd 1: 5ch (counts as tr and 2ch), (tr, 2ch) 7 times in ring, sl st in 3rd ch of t-ch to join—8 2ch spaces made. Fasten off.

Rnd 2: Join A in any 2ch space, 8ch, sl st in 4th ch from hook for picot, 5ch, sl st in 4th ch from hook for

picot, *tr in next 2ch space, work Picot of (5ch, sl st in 4th ch from hook) twice, 1ch; rep from * around, sl st in 3rd ch of 8ch t-ch to join— 16 picots made. Fasten off.

Rnd 3: Join B in 1ch between any 2 picots, 1ch, dc in first 1ch space, *7ch, skip next (picot, tr, picot), dc in 1ch space between next 2 picots; rep from * around, omitting last dc, sl st in first dc to join—8 7ch loop made.

HALLEY'S COMET MEDALLION

BRIAR ROSE MEDALLION

CELTIC MOTIF

Rnd 4: Sl st in first ch of next 7ch loop, 1ch, work (dc, htr, 9 tr, htr, dc) in each 7ch loop around, sl st in first dc to join—8 petals made. Fasten off.

HALLEY'S COMET (HC—make 4) With B, 4ch, join with sl st to form ring.

Rnd 1: 5ch (counts as tr and 2ch), (tr, 2ch) 7 times in ring, sl st in 3rd ch of 5ch t-ch to join—8 2ch spaces made. Fasten off.

Rnd 2: 3ch (counts as tr), 3 tr in next 2ch space, *tr in next tr, 3 tr in next space; rep from * around, sl st in top of 3ch t-ch to join—32 sts made. Fasten off.

Rnd 3: Join E in first st, 1ch, work a dc Spike over first st as foll: insert hook from front to back in next cor-responding st in Rnd 1 directly below, draw up loop to height of current rnd, yo, draw yarn through both loops on hook; work picot (3ch, insert hook down through top of dc just made and sl st to close), *dc in next st, 2 dc in next st, dc in next st** dc Spike in next st 2 rows below, work picot; rep from * around, ending last rep at **, sl st in first dc Spike to join. Fasten off.

hat

Make 1 Briar Rose Medallion.

BAND

With C (or desired colour for Band), make 81 (93) ch.

Work in Mock Rib:

Row 1 (WS): Tr in 4th ch from hook (counts as tr), tr in each ch across, turn—79 (91) sts.

Row 2: 2ch (counts as tr), skip first st, *FPdc around the post of next st, BPdc around the post of next st; rep from * across to within last 2 sts, FPdc around the post of next st, tr in top of t-ch, turn—79 (91) sts.

Row 3: 2ch (counts as tr), skip first st, *BPdc around the post of next st, FPdc around the post of next st; rep from * across to within last 2 sts, BPdc around the post of next st, tr in top of t-ch, turn—79 (91) sts. Fasten off.

CROWN

Row 4 (RS): Join D (or desired main colour) to top right edge of Band, 1ch, dc in first st, *skip 2 sts of Band, 3ch, dc in next st; rep from * across Band, turn—26 (30) 3ch loops made [13 (15) for front and 13 (15) for back—Hat will be seamed up left side edge].

Row 5: 4ch, dc in first loop, (3ch, dc) in each loop across, turn—26 (30) 3ch loops.

Row 6: Rep Row 5.

Make space for Briar Rose Medallion as foll:

RIGHT SIDE

Row 7 (WS): 4ch, dc in first loop, (3ch, dc) in each of next 15 (17) 3ch loops, turn, leaving rem sts unworked—16 (18) loops made.

Rows 8-17: Work even in Mesh Stitch Pattern on 16 (18) loops.

Shape Top of Crown as foll:

Row 18: 4ch, dc in first loop, (3ch, dc) in each of next 7 (8) loops, do not 3ch (place marker), dc in next 3ch loop, (3ch, dc) in each rem loop across, turn—1 loop decrease made; 15 (17) loops made.

Rows 19-24: 4ch, dc in first loop, (3ch, dc) in each loop across to marker, do not 3ch (place marker), dc in next 3ch loop, (3ch, dc) in each rem loop across, turn—9 (11) loops at end of last row. Fasten off.

LEFT SIDE

Row 7: With WS facing, skip 5 3ch loops to the left of last st made in Row 7 of Right Side, join D (or choice of MC) in next 3ch loop, 1ch, dc in same loop, (3ch, dc) in each rem loop across, turn—4 (6) loops made.

Rows 8-17: Work even in Mesh Stitch Pattern on 4 (6) loops.

Row 18 (dec) (RS): Do not 4ch, dc in first loop, (3ch, dc) in each of next 2 (4) loops, turn—1 decrease made; 3 (5) loops made.

Row 19: 4ch, dc in first loop, (3ch, dc) in each of next 2 loops—3 (5) loops made.

Row 20 (dec): Do not 4ch, dc in first loop, (3ch, dc) in each loop across, turn—2 (4) loops made.

Row 21: 4ch, dc in first loop, (3ch, dc) in each loop across, turn—2 (4) loops made.

Row 22 (dec): Do not 4ch, dc in first loop, (3ch, dc) in each loop across—1 (3) loops made. Do not fasten off. Drop loop from hook and hold with safety pin.

HAT ASSEMBLY

Fold Hat Band in half and with needle and thread, sew ends of Hat Band together. Fit Medallion in empty space in mesh at front and sew it to mesh around 3 sides, easing it in so that top edge is slightly above top edge of Crown Sides.

TOP ROW

Pick up dropped loop at end of Row 22 of Left Side, 4ch, (dc, 3ch) in next 3ch loop, work (dc, 3ch, skip 1.3 cm) evenly across top of Briar Rose Medallion, then work (dc, 3ch) in each loop across Right Side, ending with dc in last 3ch loop. Fasten off, leaving a sewing length. Sew Side seam.

cardigan

WAISTBAND

With A, make 131 (143, 155, 167) ch.

Row 1 (WS): Tr in 4th ch from hook (counts as tr), tr in each ch across, turn—129 (141, 153, 165) sts made.

Work Rows 2-3 of Mock Rib Stitch on 129 (141, 153, 165) sts until Waistband measures 10.2 cm from beg, ending with a WS row.

Shape Sides

Next Row: 2ch (count as tr), skip first st, work in Row 2 pattern of Mock Rib Stitch across next 34 sts, 2 FPdc around the post of next st, place marker for Beg of Back, 2 BPdc around the post of next st, work in pattern across next 55 (67, 79, 91) sts, (37 sts before end), 2 BPdc around the post of next st, place marker for End of Back, 2 FPdc around the post of next st, work in pattern across remaining 35 sts, turn—4 increases made; 133 (145, 157, 169) sts.

Work even in Mock Rib Stitch pattern for 3 rows incorporating new sts into pattern.

Next Row: Work in Mock Rib Stitch pattern, inc 1 st before and after each marker at each side—4 increases made; 137 (149, 161, 173) sts. *(Note: There should be 61 (73, 85, 97) sts between markers for Back.)*

Work even in Mock Rib Stitch pattern until Waistband measures 15.2 cm from beg, ending with a WS row.

Cont to work across 7 edge sts for Front Band as foll:

FIRST FRONT BAND

Row 1 (RS): 2ch (counts as tr), work in patt across next 5 sts, tr in next st, turn.

Work even in Mock Rib Stitch pattern on 7 sts until Front Band measures 27.9 (29.2, 30.5, 31.8) cm above end of Waistband (43.2 (44.5, 45.7, 47) cm total from bottom of Waistband). Fasten off.

SECOND FRONT BAND

With RS facing, join A in last row of Waistband, 7 sts in from other edge. Work same as First Front Band. Fasten off.

BACK

Row 1 (RS): With RS facing, join B with sl st in last row of Waistband in first st to the left of first side marker for Back, 1ch, dc in same st, *3ch, skip next 2 sts, dc in next st; rep from * across to next marker, turn—20 (24, 28, 32) 3ch loops made.

Row 2: 4ch, dc in first loop, (3ch, dc) in each loop across, turn—20 (24, 28, 32) 3ch loops.

Rows 3–6: Rep Row 2 for Mesh Stitch pattern.

Inc by 1 loop at each edge over next 2 rows as foll:

Row 7 (inc) (RS): 4ch, dc in first loop, (3ch, dc) in first loop (inc),

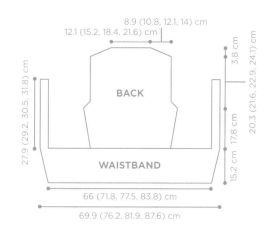

CHART KEY

AW = Amanda Whorl
CM = Celtic Motif
BR = Briar Rose
HC = Halley's Comet
C = Rnds 1-2 of Celtic Motif
▨ = Mesh St fill-in areas as necessary

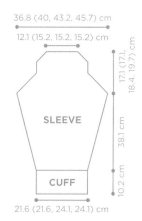

(3ch, dc) in each loop across, turn—21 (25, 29, 33) 3ch loops.

Row 8 (inc) (WS): 4ch, dc in first loop, (3ch, dc) in first loop (inc), (3ch, dc) in each loop across, turn—22 (26, 30, 34) 3ch loops.

Rep Rows 3–8 once—24 (28, 32, 36) 3ch loops at end of last row.

Work even in Mesh Stitch pattern until Back measures 17.8 cm above Waistband (33 cm from bottom of Waistband), ending with a WS row.

Shape Armhole

Next Row (dec) (RS): Do not 4ch, dc in first 3ch loop, (3ch, dc) in each loop across, turn—1 loop dec made—23 (27, 31, 35) 3ch loops.

Next Row (dec) (WS): Do not 4ch, dc in first 3ch loop, (3ch, dc) in each loop across, turn—1 loop dec made—22 (26, 30, 34) 3ch loops.

Rep last 2 rows once—20 (24, 28, 32) 3ch loops at end of last row.

Work even in Mesh Stitch pattern until Armhole measures 20.3 (21.6, 22.9, 24.1) cm from beg.

Shape Shoulder

Row 1: 4ch, dc in first loop, (3ch, dc) in each loop across to within last 3 (4, 5, 6) loops, turn, leaving remaining sts unworked—17 (20, 23, 26) 3ch loops made.

Row 2: Rep Row 1–14 (16, 18, 20) 3ch loops made.

Row 3: 4ch, dc in first loop, (3ch, dc) in each loop across to within last 3 loops, turn, leaving remaining sts unworked—11 (13, 15, 17) 3ch loops made.

Row 4: Rep Row 3–8 (10, 12, 14) 3ch loops made.

(Note: 6 [7, 8, 9] loops decreased each side for shoulder.)

CUFF

With A, ch 45 (45, 51, 51).

Row 1 (WS): Tr in 4th ch from hook (counts as tr), tr in each ch across, turn—43 (43, 49, 49) sts made.

Work Rows 2–3 of Mock Rib Stitch on 43 (43, 49, 49) sts until Cuff measures 10.2 cm from beg, ending with a WS row. Fasten off.

Next Row (RS): With RS facing, join B in top right-hand st of Band, 1ch, dc in first st, *3ch, skip next 2 sts, dc in next st; rep from * across to next marker, turn—14 (14, 16, 16) 3ch loops made.

Next Row: 4ch, dc in first loop, (3ch, dc) in each loop across, turn—14 (14, 16, 16) 3ch loops.

Work even in Mesh Stitch pattern for 4 more rows.

Inc by 1 loop at each edge over next 2 rows as foll:

Next Row (inc) (RS): 4ch, dc in first loop, (3ch, dc) in first loop (inc), (3ch, dc) in each loop across, turn—15 (15, 17, 17) 3ch loops.

Next Row (inc) (WS): 4ch, dc in first loop, (3ch, dc) in first loop (inc), (3ch, dc) in each loop across, turn—16 (16, 18, 18) 3ch loops.

Work even in Mesh Stitch pattern for 6 (6, 6, 5) rows. Then work 2-row inc—18 (18, 20, 20) 3ch loops at end of last row.

Rep last 8 (8, 8, 7) rows 3 (4, 4, 5) times—24 (26, 28, 30) 3ch loops at end of last row.

Work even in Mesh Stitch pattern until Sleeve measures 48.3 cm from beg (38.1 cm from cuff), ending with a WS row.

CAP

Next Row (dec) (RS): Do not 4ch, dc in first 3ch loop, (3ch, dc) in each loop across, turn—1 loop dec made—23 (25, 27, 29) 3ch loops.

Next Row (dec) (WS): Do not 4ch, dc in first 3ch loop, (3ch, dc) in each loop across, turn—1 loop dec made—22 (24, 26, 28) 3ch loops.

Rep last 2 rows 5 times—12 (14, 16, 18) 3ch loops at end of last row.

Work even in Mesh Stitch pattern for 6 rows, then dec 1 loop at beg of each of next 4 (4, 6, 8) rows—8 (10, 10, 10) 3ch loops at end of last row. *(Note: 22 [22, 24, 26] rows total in Sleeve Cap.)* Fasten off.

COLLAR

With A, make 91 (103, 115, 127) ch.

Row 1 (WS): Tr in 4th ch from hook (counts as tr), tr in each ch across, turn—89 (101, 113, 125) sts made.

Rows 2–3: Work even in Mock Rib Stitch pattern on 89 (101, 113, 125) sts.

Shape Decorative Top Edge

Row 4 (RS): 2ch, skip first st, work tr3tog across next 3 sts as foll: working first half-closed tr as a FPdc in next st, work next half-closed tr as a BPdc in next st, work last half-closed tr as a FPdc in next st, yo, complete cluster, work in Mock Rib Stitch pattern across to within last 4 sts, work tr3tog across next 3 sts as before, tr in top of t-ch, turn.

Row 5 (WS): 2ch, skip first st, skip first leg of tr3tog, FPdc around the post of next post (centre st of tr3tog), skip next leg of tr3tog, *FPdc around the post of next st, 2 BPdc around the post of next st; rep from * across to within last 2 sts, skip first leg of tr3tog, FPdc around the post of next post (centre st of tr3tog), skip next leg of tr3tog, tr in top of t-ch. Fasten off.

FINISHING

Sew Sleeve seams. With centre top of Sleeves at top of Back shoulders, sew back edge of Sleeve Caps to Back Armholes. Pin centre of Collar to centre Back Neck and arrange so that it just meets inner corner of top Front Band; baste Collar in place along 8 (10, 12, 14) 3ch loops of Back Neck edge, to help with arranging Medallions.

Arrange and Sew Medallions

You may wish to try on to estimate how much area will need to be filled in on Fronts. *(Note: Bust measurements have been determined based on measurements of 17.8 [19.1, 20.3, 21.6] cm for each Front Medallion area.)* Allow for 2.5 cm at centre front to be added by hook and eye closure. You can use cloth to make a template or use Back to gauge outlines of front silhouette. Arrange Medallions on each Front as shown on Front schematic. The schematic is just a guide; feel free to improvise. Medallions will stretch a great deal without distorting them terribly, so to eliminate fill-in areas, join more edges of the Medallions than seem to fit naturally. The Amanda Whorl will lap over left Sleeve Cap. Using needle and thread, sew Medallion edges together from RS using small whip st toward back of work that will be hidden in seam. Also sew Medallions to side edge of Back and Sleeve and to inside edge of Front Band. Sew Collar in place across neck edge.

MESH FILL-INS

Fill in remaining areas using B and Mesh Stitch, working in the direction of the closest straight edge—e.g., join to Front Band with sl st, 1ch, dc in same st, *3ch, skip 1.3 cm span of Band, dc in next st on band; rep from * as needed, turn and cont in Mesh pattern, decreasing or increasing as necessary to fill an area without overlapping medallions. Fasten off. Use needle and thread to sew edges of fill-in Mesh areas to surrounding areas.

Sew hooks and eyes to Front Bands (with hooks on right front band facing outward) placing one 6 mm below top edge, one 6 mm above bottom edge, and 9 remaining hooks and eyes evenly spaced between.

solomon knot flower shawl

OVERVIEW

Shawl is worked from right shoulder edge, where three flowers are linked together with a network of knot stitches. Shawl is worked off the edge of assembled flowers in Solomon Knot pattern to left shoulder edge. Fourth flower is sewn to inner corner of final edge to serve as a "button" to be pulled through "buttonhole" of open stitch pattern area at right shoulder. Then a few fringes are added to first edge.

FLOWER (make 4)

CENTRE PETALS

With A, make 5ch, join with sl st to form ring.

Rnd 1 (RS): 5ch, htr in first ch from hook (for picot), 4ch, sl st in first ch of ring, (sl st, 5ch, htr in first ch from hook, 4ch, sl st) in each ch around, sl st in first ch to join—5 petals made.

Rnd 2: *Ch 16, dc in centre ring between next 2 petals; rep from * around—5ch-16 loops made. Fasten off A.

OUTER PETALS

Rnd 3: With RS facing, join B in back of first dc in Rnd 2, working behind

One size fits most adults.

MEASUREMENTS

Approximately 25.4 cm wide x 106.7 cm long excluding Flower button closure

YARN

Trendsetter "Dolcino" (75% acrylic/26% poly-amide) flat ribbon yarn

3 balls (1.75 oz/50 g; 99 yd/90 m) in #103 caramel (A)

Needful yarns "Modigliani" (100% merino) aran weight tubular yarn

4 balls (1.75 oz/50 g; 71 yd/65 m) in #03 taupe heather (B)

HOOKS

6.5 mm (US K/10 ¹/₂) or size to match gauge

NOTIONS

Optional: safety pins and muslin or scrap cloth to use as template for assembly

GAUGE

First 4 rnds of Flower = 11.4 cm in diameter. Flower = 19.1 cm in diameter. With 1 strand each of A and B held together, 2 loops of (dc, 2 knot sts) = 11.4 cm; 2 rows in Solomon Knot stitch of Shawl = 15.2 cm

Always check and MATCH gauge for best results.

petals in Rnds 1 and 2, *4ch, dc on the back of next dc between petals; rep from * around—5 4ch loops made.

Rnd 4: Sl st in top of dc in Rnd 2, *2ch, 3 tr in next 4ch loop, 2ch, sl st in next dc in Rnd 2; rep from * around—5 petals made.

Rnd 5: *8ch, skip next petal, sl st in back of sl st between next 2 petals; rep from * around—5 8ch loops made.

Rnd 6: *7 tr in next 8ch loop, sl st in next sl st; rep from * around—5 petals made.

Rnd 7: *8ch, skip next 3 tr, sl st in next tr, 8ch, skip next 3 tr, sl st in next sl st; rep from * around—10 8ch loops made.

STAMEN

With WS of Flower facing, sl st in back of each round to reach centre ring of flower, sl st in centre ring. Drop loop from hook. Turn Flower to RS, insert hook in centre ring and pick up dropped loop to work Stamen around centre ring from RS. *(Note: 6 sts will be worked in Stamen Rnd, work sts evenly spaced around centre ring.)*

Stamen Rnd: *Work bullion st in centre ring, sl st in centre ring; rep from * twice, working sts evenly space around. Fasten off.

SHAWL ASSEMBLY

Solomon Knot Joining Network: This is a "free-form" design. Feel "free" to use your own imagination when arranging and joining the Flowers or follow the directions given. A diagram and instructions are provided

special stitches

KNOT STITCH (KNOT ST) (see page 77)
Draw up a loop (3.2 cm loop for shorter knot st or 6.4 cm for longer knot st), yo, draw yarn through long loop on hook (ch made), insert hook in single strand (bottom part) of long loop just made, yo, draw yarn through loop, yo, draw through 2 loops on hook (dc made to complete knot st).

(Note: This shawl has an organic look, so as you link pieces with knot stitch vary the length of the loops between 3.2 cm to 6.4 cm to serve your needs; when working Solomon Knot Stitch pattern the edge knots are traditionally 2/3 the length of the knots within the middle of the row to keep fabric even along the edges, so make these shorter and the middle ones longer as indicated.)

BULLION STITCH

Wrap yarn 4 times around shaft of hook, insert hook in st and pull up a loop, yo and draw through every loop on hook *(Tip: I use left thumb and index finger to pinch the tight wraps and drop them off the hook one by one while pulling the hook through).*

FLOWER

STITCH KEY

⚬ = chain (ch)

• = slip st (sl st)

X = double crochet (dc)

T = half treble crochet (htr)

⊤ = treble crochet (tr)

to show the sequence of knot sts and dc used to connect the first three Flowers. Follow the numerical path of knot sts. The instructions will occasionally indicate numbers to help you find the path. Sections are shown in different colors to help distinguish the path. Red section (numbered 1 through 20) begins with a fringe length, then is worked around Flower I, then fastened off. Purple section (numbered 1 through 19) begins with a fringe length, then is worked around the Second Flower, joining it to Flower I. Without fastening off, begin working Turquoise section (numbered 20 through 47): Work around Flower III, while joining it to Flowers I and II, then continue around the rest of Flower III. Without fastening off, continue on to Black section which shows the first 3 rows of the Shawl. Row 2 will be repeated for the length of the Shawl. Unless otherwise stated, all knot sts within the Joining Network will be worked to desired length, adjusting as needed to reach joining points and to keep the piece laying flat.

Flower I Rnd: Begin Red Section: With 1 strand each of A and B held together as one, make a slipknot leaving 10.2 cm tail for fringe, work 3 knot sts, dc in any 8ch loop of Flower I (#4), with WS facing, (work longer knot st, dc in next 8ch loop) 4 times, (2 shorter knot sts, dc in next 8ch loop) 5 times, work 2 shorter knot sts, dc in dc in first 8ch loop where rnd began (#20). Fasten off.

Arrange Flowers I, II, and III as shown—you may find it helpful to arrange flowers on a cloth and pin centre of each flower to cloth, leaving edge loops free (so you can lift loops up to work from WS).

Flower II Joining Row: Begin Purple Section: With 1 strand each of A and B held together as one, make a slipknot leaving 10.2 cm tail for fringe, work 3 knot sts, dc in any 8ch loop of Flower (#4), with WS facing, work knot st, dc

in dc between next 2 knots on Flower I, knot st, dc in next 8ch loop of Flower II (#6), knot st, dc in dc between next 2 knot sts on Flower I, knot st, dc in same 8ch loop of Flower II (#8), work 2 knot sts, dc in dc between next 2 knot sts on Flower I (#10), turn, work 2 knot sts, skip last 2 knot sts made, dc in dc between next 2 knot sts (#12), then cont to work on WS around Flower II: knot st, dc in next 8ch loop of Flower II, (work 2 knot sts, dc in next 8ch loop of Flower II) twice, work longer knot st, dc in next 8ch loop, turn, work longer knot st, skip last 2 knot sts made, dc in dc between next 2 knot sts (#19).

Flower III Joining Row: Begin Turquoise Section: work 2 knot sts, with WS facing, dc in any 8ch loop of Flower III (#21), knot st, skip last 2 knots sts made, dc in dc between next 2 knot sts (#22), knot st, dc in same 8ch loop of Flower III holding last dc (#23), knot st, dc in dc between next 2 knot loops of Flower II, knot st, dc in next 8ch loop of Flower III, knot st, dc in dc between next 2 knot sts (#26), knot st, dc in next 8ch loop of Flower III, knot st, dc in dc in 8ch loop of Flower I (#28), knot st, dc in next 8ch loop of Flower III, knot st, dc in dc between next 2 knot sts of Flower I, knot st, dc in same 8ch loop of Flower III (#31), knot st, dc in dc between next 2 knot sts of Flower I, work 2 knot sts, dc in next 8ch loop of Flower III (#34), work 3 knot sts, dc in dc in 8ch loop of Flower I (#37), work 2 knot sts, dc in dc between next 2 knots on Flower I, knot st, skip last 2 knot sts made, dc in dc between next 2 knot sts, knot st, skip next 3 knot sts, dc in dc between next 2 knot sts (#41), knot st, dc in next 8ch loop on Flower III (#42), then cont to work around Flower III: (knot st, dc in next 8ch loop of Flower III) 4 times, knot st, dc in dc between 2 knot sts below (#47), turn to begin Shawl Pattern.

Begin Black Section

Row 1: Work 2 knot sts, skip last 3 knot sts made, dc in dc between next 2 knot sts (#49), (work 2 longer knot sts, skip 2 knot sts, dc in dc between next 2 knot sts) twice, turn.

Row 2: Work 2 short knot sts and 1 longer knot st, skip last 4 knot sts made, dc in dc between next 2 knot sts (#56), (work 2 longer knot sts, skip next 2 knot sts, dc in dc between next 2 knot sts) twice, work 2 longer knot sts, skip next knot st, dc in next dc (#62), turn.

Row 3: Work 2 short knot sts and 1 longer knot st, skip last 4 knot sts made, dc in dc between next 2 knot sts (#65), (work 2 longer knot sts, skip next 2 knot sts, dc in dc between next 2 knot sts) 3 times, turn.

Rep Row 3 for Solomon Knot stitch pattern until piece measures approximately 61 cm from beg of Shawl Pattern or 106.7 cm from end to end.

FINISHING
Begin Green Sections

First Fringe: With 1 strand each of A and B held together as one, make a slipknot leaving 10.2 cm tail for fringe, work 1 knot st, dc in designated dc (#6) of Flower I. Fasten off.

Second Fringe: With 1 strand each of A and B held together as one, make a slipknot leaving 10.2 cm tail for fringe, work 2 knot sts, dc in next designated dc (#5) of Flower I. Fasten off.

Third Fringe: With 1 strand each of A and B held together as one, make a slipknot leaving 10.2 cm tail for fringe, work 3 knot sts, dc in next designated 8ch loop (to the right of #4) of Flower II. Fasten off.

Attach rem 4th Flower to upper right corner edge of shawl—when folded this will be neck edge. To fasten, wrap shawl around shoulders. Bring this 4th Flower "button" through open stitch area.

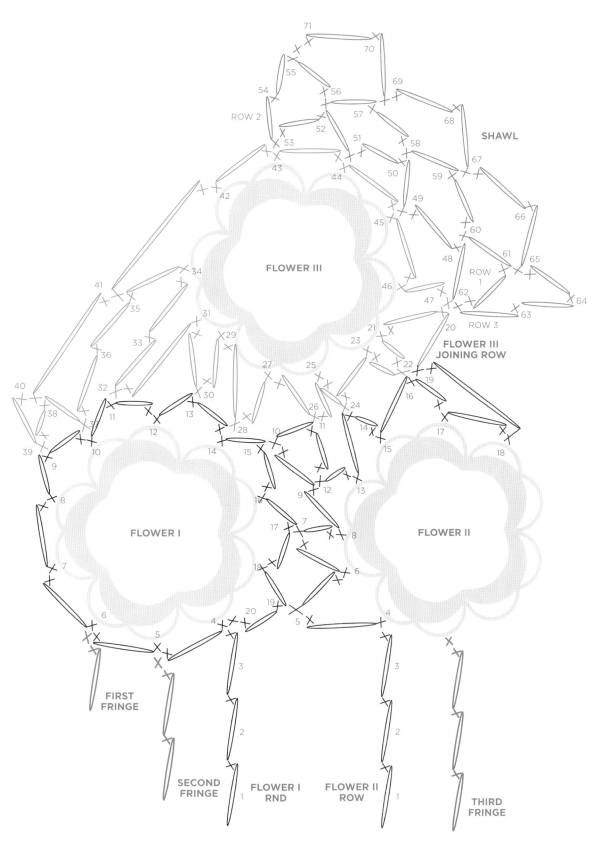

SOLOMON'S KNOT JOINING NETWORK

lazy wheels coat

OVERVIEW

Body of coat is worked in one piece to armhole in Chevron stitch; the stitch pattern is altered to shape waist and at top bodice to even out the scallops in the fabric. Lazy Wheels are worked separately and sewn together for Train.

COAT

Make 84 (94) ch plus 3 for t-ch.

Row 1: Tr in 4th ch from hook, tr in each of next 2 (3) ch, *tr2tog over next 2 ch, tr in each of next 3 ch, 2 tr in each of next 2 ch, tr in each of next 3 ch, tr2tog over next 2 ch, tr in each of next 4 (6) ch; rep from * 4 times, ending last rep with tr in each of last 3 (4) ch, turn—82 (92) sts made.

Row 2: 3ch (counts as tr), tr in each of next 2 (3) sts, *tr2tog over next 2 sts, tr in each of next 3 sts, 2 tr in each of next 2 sts, tr in each of next 3 sts, tr2tog over next 2 sts, tr in each of next 4 (6) sts; rep from * 4 times, ending last rep with tr in each of last 3 (4) sts, turn—82 (92) sts made. *(Note: Stitch count remains even as same number of decreases and increases are made.)*

Rep Row 2 for Chevron Stitch I until Coat measures 43.2 (38.1) cm from beg or desired length, ending with a WS row. *(Note: To adjust for your stature, subtract 2.5 cm for each 2.5 cm under 1.75 metre you measure.)*

Shape Waist

Next Row (dec) (RS): 3ch (counts as tr), tr in each of next 2 (3) sts, tr2tog over next 2 sts, *tr in each of next

---

Shown in smaller size

Adjust length where indicated in pattern for stature, shown on 1.75 metre model.

MEASUREMENTS

Bust: 96.5 (109.2) cm overlap of front flap allows for adjusting fit

Hips: 104.1 (116.8) cm with front edges meeting

Length as shown: 137.2 cm without gravity

YARN

Needful Yarns/King "Van Dyck" (46% wool/39% acrylic/15% alpaca) bulky heather yarn

16 (20) balls (3.5 oz/ 100 g; 117 yd/107 m) in #102 light gray

HOOKS

8 mm (US L/11) or size to match gauge

NOTIONS

Optional: safety pins and fabric (muslin or old sheet) to use in assembly

Tapestry needle

2 horse bit–shaped silver buckles 3.2 cm tall, 6.4 cm long (M&J Trimming)

GAUGE

8 sts and 4 rows = 10.2 cm (do not count the peak of chevron but measure over straight rows) in Chevron Stitch I Pattern

(Note: Sizing is done by adding 2 extra sts to each rep in stitch pattern.)

Lazy Wheel = 10.2 cm in diameter

Always check and MATCH gauge for best results.

3 sts, 2 tr in each of next 2 sts, tr in each of next 3 sts**, (tr2tog over next 2 sts) twice, tr in each of next (0) 2 sts, (tr2tog over next 2 sts) twice; rep from * 4 times, ending last rep at **, tr2tog in next 2 sts, tr in each of last 3 (4) sts, turn—74 (84) sts (8 sts decreased across row).

Next Row: 3ch (counts as tr), tr in each of next 2 (3) sts, *tr2tog over next 2 sts, tr in each of next 3 sts, 2 tr in each of next 2 sts, tr in each of next 3 sts, tr2tog in next 2 sts, tr in each of next 2 (4) sts; rep from * 4 times, ending last rep with tr in each of last 3 (4) sts, turn—74 (84) sts.

Rep last row for Chevron Stitch II. Work in est pattern for 6 more rows or until piece measures 20.3 cm from beg of Waist Shaping, ending with a WS row.

Divide for Armholes

RIGHT FRONT

Work in Chevron Stitch II over first 23 (26) sts as follows:

Row 1: 3ch (counts as tr), tr in each of next 2 (3) sts, *tr2tog over next 2 sts, tr in each of next 3 sts, 2 tr in each of next 2 sts, tr in each of next 3 sts, tr2tog over next 2 sts, tr in each of next 2 (4) sts, tr2tog over next 2 sts, tr in each of next 3 sts, 2 tr in next st, turn, leaving rem sts unworked—23 (26) sts.

Row 2: 3ch (counts as tr), tr in same st as 3ch, tr in each of next 3 sts, tr2tog over next 2 sts, tr in each of next 2 (4) sts, tr2tog over next 2 sts, tr in each of next 3 sts, 2 tr in each of next 2 sts, tr in each of next 3 sts, tr2tog in next 2 sts, tr in each of next 3 (4) sts, turn—23 (26) sts.

Cont in est pattern on 23 (26) sts until Right Front measures 15.2 (20.3)

cm from beg of Armhole, ending with a WS row (6 [8] rows have been worked). Begin Chevron Stitch III as follows:

Next Row (RS): Sl st over first 10 (11) sts (centre of chevron rep) (9 [10] sts decreased for neck flap), 2ch, skip first tr, work tr in next tr but pull last loop tog with turning ch as for tr2tog (counts as tr2tog), tr in each of next 4 (5) sts, 2 tr in each of next 2 sts, tr in each of next 4 (5) sts, tr2tog over next 2 sts, turn—14 (16) sts.

Next Row (WS): 2ch, skip first tr, work tr in next tr but pull last loop tog with turning ch as for tr2tog (counts as tr2tog), tr in each of next 4 (5) tr, 2 tr in each of next 2 sts, tr in each of next 4 (5) sts, tr2tog over next 2 sts, turn—14 (16) sts.

Next Row: Rep last row. Fasten off.

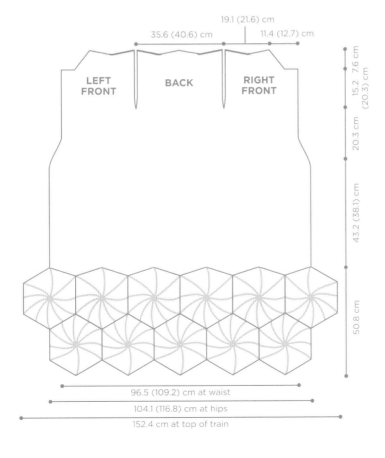

19.1 (21.6) cm

35.6 (40.6) cm · 11.4 (12.7) cm

LEFT FRONT · BACK · RIGHT FRONT

15.2 7.6 cm (20.3) cm

20.3 cm

43.2 (38.1) cm

50.8 cm

96.5 (109.2) cm at waist

104.1 (116.8) cm at hips

152.4 cm at top of train

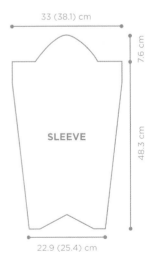

33 (38.1) cm

7.6 cm

SLEEVE

48.3 cm

22.9 (25.4) cm

special stitches

CRAB STITCH (REVERSE DC)

Working from left to right, insert hook in next st to the right, yo, draw yarn through st, yo, draw yarn through 2 loops on hook. (The stitch will have a raised and twisted look.)

CHEVRON STITCH I

(multiple of 16 (18) plus 2, plus 2 ch for tch)

Row 1: Tr in 4th ch from hook, tr in each of next 2 (3) ch, *tr2tog over next 2 ch, tr in each of next 3 ch, 2 tr in each of next 2 ch, tr in each of next 3 ch, tr2tog over next 2 ch, tr in each of next 4 (6) ch; rep from * across, ending last rep with tr in each of last 3 (4) ch, turn.

Row 2: 3ch (counts as tr), tr in each of next 2 (3) sts, *tr2tog over next 2 sts, tr in each of next 3 sts, 2 tr in each of next 2 sts, tr in each of next 3 sts, tr2tog over next 2 sts, tr in each of next 4 (6) sts; rep from * across, ending last rep with tr in each of last 3 (4) sts, turn.

Rep Row 2 for Chevron Stitch I Pattern.

LAZY WHEEL

(Note: Wheel is worked in 10 segments of 2 rows each, which are worked sideways and repeated around a centre circle—see diagram.)

Ch 17, sl st in 8th ch from hook to form centre ring, leaving 9 ch for foundation ch of Segment 1.

Segment 1: Row 1: Working across 9ch foundation ch, dc in next ch, htr in next ch, tr in next ch, 2 tr in next ch, tr in next ch, 2 dtr in next ch, dtr in next ch, 2 trtr in next ch, trtr in last ch, do not turn—12 sts made.

Row 2: Working from left to right in front loops of sts, work Crab stitch in each st across to centre ring, sl st in centre ring.

Segment 2: Row 1: Working behind Crab stitch row in the back loops of sts in previous row, dc in next st, htr in next st, tr in next st, 2 tr in next st, tr in next st, 2 dtr in next st, dtr in next st, 2 trtr in next st, trtr in last st, do not turn—12 sts made.

Row 2: Working from left to right in front loops of sts, work Reverse dc in each st across to centre ring, sl st in centre ring.

Segments 3–10: Work as for Segment 2.

When all 10 segments have been made, turn work to WS and sl st foundation ch together with back of final Crab stitch row over 9 sts to join. Fasten off.

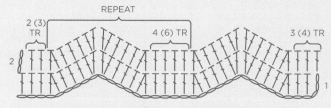

REDUCED SAMPLE OF CHEVRON STITCH I

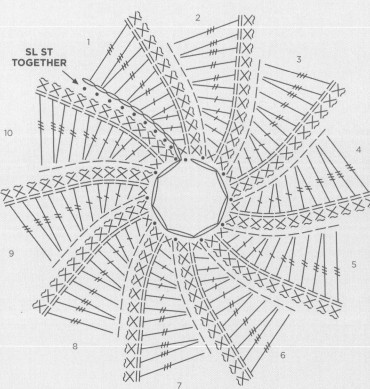

LAZY WHEEL MOTIF

STITCH KEY

⬭ = chain (ch)

• = slip st (sl st)

X = double crochet (dc)

X̃ = crab stitch

┬ = half treble crochet (htr)

┬ = treble crochet (tr)

┬ = double treble crochet (dtr)

┬ = triple treble crochet (trtr)

— = worked in back loop

BACK

Row 1: With RS facing, join yarn in first st to the left of last st made in Row 1 of Right Front, working Chevron Stitch II across next 28 (32) sts as follows: 3ch (counts as tr), tr in same st as 3ch, tr in each of next 3 sts, tr2tog over next 2 sts, tr in each of next 2 (4) sts, tr2tog over next 2 sts, tr in each of next 3 sts, 2 tr in each of next 2 sts, tr in each of next 3 sts, tr2tog in next 2 sts, tr in each of next 2 (4) sts, tr2tog over next 2 sts, tr in each of next 3 sts, 2 tr in next st, turn, leaving rem sts unworked—28 (32 sts).

Cont in est pattern on 28 (32) sts until Back measures 15.2 (20.3) cm from beg of Armhole, ending with a WS row (6 [8] rows have been worked). Begin Chevron Stitch III as follows:

Next Row (RS): 2ch, skip first tr, work tr in next tr but pull last loop tog with turning ch as for tr2tog (counts as tr2tog), tr in each of next 4 (5) sts, 2 tr in each of next 2 sts, tr in each of next 4 (5) sts, (tr2tog over next 2 sts) twice, tr in each of next 4 (5) sts, 2 tr in each of next 2 sts, tr in each of next 4 (5) sts, tr2tog over next 2 sts, turn—28 (32 sts). *(Note: Stitch count remains even as same number of decreases and increases are made.)*

Rep last row twice. Fasten off.

LEFT FRONT

Row 1: With RS facing, join yarn in first st to the left of last st made in Row 1 of Back, working Chevron Stitch II across last 23 (26) sts as follows: 3ch (counts as tr), tr in same st as 3ch, tr in each of next 3 sts, tr2tog over next 2 sts, tr in each of next 2 (4) sts, tr2tog over next 2 sts, tr in each of next 3 sts, 2 tr in each of next 2 sts, tr in each of next 3 sts, tr2tog over next 2 sts, tr in each of next 3 (4) sts, turn.

Cont in est pattern on 23 (26) sts until Left Front measures 15.2 (20.3) cm from beg of Armhole, ending with a WS row (6 [8] rows have been worked). Begin Chevron Stitch III as follows:

Next Row (RS): 2ch, skip first tr, work tr in next tr but pull last loop tog with turning ch as for tr2tog (counts as tr2tog), tr in each of next 4 (5) sts, 2 tr in each of next 2 sts, tr in each of next 4 (5) sts, tr2tog over next 2 sts, turn, leaving rem 9 (10) sts unworked for neck flap—14 (16) sts.

Next Row (WS): 2ch, skip first tr, work tr in next tr but pull last loop tog with turning ch as for tr2tog (counts as tr2tog), tr in each of next 4 (5) tr, 2 tr in each of next 2 sts, tr in each of next 4 (5) sts, tr2tog over next 2 sts, turn—14 (16) sts.

Next Row: Rep last row. Fasten off.

SLEEVE (make 2)

Starting at cuff edge, ch 20 (22).

Row 1: Tr in 4th ch from hook, tr in each of next 1 (2) ch, tr2tog over next 2 ch, tr in each of next 3 ch, 2 tr in each of next 2 ch, tr in each of next 3 ch, tr2tog in next 2 ch, tr in each of last 3 (4) ch, turn—18 (20) sts made.

Row 2: 3ch (counts as tr), tr in each of next 2 (3) sts, tr2tog over next 2 sts, tr in each of next 3 sts, 2 tr in each of next 2 sts, tr in each of next 3 sts, tr2tog over next 2 sts, tr in each of last 3 (4) sts, turn—18 (20) sts made.

Rep Row 2 in Chevron Stitch I, inc 1 tr at each end every 4th (3rd) row 4 (5) times, maintaining one chevron at centre of Sleeve—26 (30) sts at end of last inc row.

Work even in est pattern until Sleeve measures 48.3 cm from beg (centre has chevron peak that forms sleeve cap). Fasten off.

TRAIN

Make 11 Lazy Wheel Motifs. Arrange in formation shown on diagram with 6 wheels across top tier and 5 across bottom, with indented pinwheel-like segments intermeshing like cogs in machine and segment ridges aligning. Fit top edge of top tier as evenly as possible across bottom edge of Coat. You may find it helpful to pin arrangement down to fabric and leave edges free to sew. Use yarn needle and 1 strand yarn to sew motif edges together, work from RS but toward bottom of sts working side to side, alternating 1 stitch on each piece (Mattress stitch).

FINISHING

Sew sleeve seams. Sew shoulder seams across 9 (10) sts on Fronts and Back, leaving 10 (12) sts open for back neck, 5 (6) sts open at each front neck. Set in sleeves (peak of chevron provides ease like sleeve cap) and attach from WS with dc all around armhole.

SWEATER EDGING

With RS facing, join yarn on Left Front edge above top of Train, 1ch, working from left to right, rev dc evenly across Left Front edge, around neck edge and down Right Front edge to top of Train. Fasten off.

Overlap Right Front over Left Front and sew one side of one buckle to top edge of Right Front neck flap and one side of second buckle 6 (8) rows down on Right Front edge. Try on and sew other side of buckles to correspond, using photo as a guide.

Some of the techniques I've presented in this book are novel, but the instructions have been written in standard crochet pattern language. Here are some tips to help you get the best results. On page 141 is a glossary of terms and abbreviations. All efforts have been made to ensure that the instructions are comprehensive and error-free. Please follow them carefully. Nevertheless, mistakes do happen—if you believe you've found one, please write to me by way of my publisher (Stewart, Tabori & Chang, 115 W. 18th St., New York, NY 10011) so I may address it.

CRAB ST
Page 24 Patch Pocket Skirt
Page 134 Lazy Wheels Coat

Step 1: With right side facing, working from left to right, insert hook in next st to the right.

Step 2: Yo, draw yarn through st.

Step 3: Yo, draw yarn through 2 loops on hook (1 crab st or 1 reverse dc made).

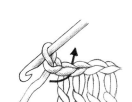

Step 1

Step 2

Step 3

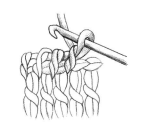

Completed Stitches

KNOT ST
Page 76 Knotwork Socks
Page 130 Solomon Flower Shawl

Step 1: Draw up a long loop on hook to desired length, yo, draw yarn through long loop on hook.

Step 2: Insert hook in single strand (bottom part) of long loop just made, yo, draw yarn through loop.

Step 3: Yo, draw through 2 loops on hook (knot st made).

Step 1

Step 2

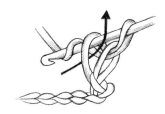

Step 3

MARGUERITE CLUSTER
Page 97 Marguerite Jacket

First Row

Step 1: Draw up a 1.9 cm loop in 2nd, 3rd and 5th ch from hook.

Step 2: Yo, draw yarn through 4 loops on hook (cluster made), 1ch to secure (first M3C made).

Step 3: Draw up a 1.9 cm loop in 1ch space (made to secure last M3C), draw up a 1.9 cm loop in base of last spike of last M3C, skip 1 ch, draw up a 1.9 cm loop in next ch, yo, draw yarn through 4 loops on hook.

Step 4: 1ch to secure (M3C made).

Step 1

Step 2

Step 3

Step 4

SINGLE LEG CLOVER CLUSTER (SLC)
Page 101 Clover Fan Jacket

Step 1: Yo, insert hook in next st, yo, draw up a 2.5 cm loop (3 loops on hook).

Step 2: Yo, insert hook in same st, yo, draw up a 2.5 cm loop (5 loops on hook).

Step 3: Yo, draw through 4 loops on hook (2 loops on hook).

Step 4: Yo, draw through 2 loops on hook.

Steps 1 and 2

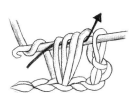

S

Step 4

Completed Stitch

DOUBLE LEG CLOVER CLUSTER (DLC)
Page 101 Clover Fan Jacket

Step 1: Work Steps 1 and 2 of Single Leg Clover Cluster in designated st.

Step 2: Rep Steps 1 and 2 of Single Leg Clover Cluster in next designated st (9 loops on hook).

Step 3: Yo, draw through 8 loops on hook (2 loops on hook).

Step 4: Yo, draw through 2 loops on hook.

Steps 1 and 2

Step 3

Step 4

Completed Stitch

Page 122 Medallion Cardigan and Hat

Step 1: Yo, insert hook from front to back to front again around the post of next st.

Step 2: Yo, draw up a loop, (yo, draw through 2 loops on hook) twice.

Page 122 Medallion Cardigan and Hat

Step 1: Yo, insert hook from back to front to back again around the post of next st.

Step 2: Yo, draw up a loop, (yo, draw through 2 loops on hook) twice.

Step 1

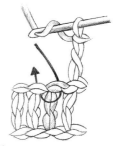

Step 1

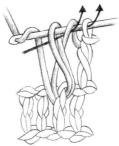

Step 2

Step 2

Completed Stitch

Completed Stitch

TERMS AND ABBREVIATIONS

approx = approximately

back loop only = insert hook into the half of the stitch furthest from you

beg = begin, beginning

bet = between

blocking = the use of steam, water and/or pins to flatten pieces to measurements. Consult the yarn band for recommended treatment before applying any blocking method.

BPdc = back post double crochet

ch = chain

crab stitch = reverse double crochet (see page 138)

dc = double crochet

dec = decrease, decreasing

dtr = double treble crochet

FPdc = front post double crochet

front loop only = insert hook into the half of the stitch closest to you

gauge = tension of the work. Make sure to measure gauge as specified in pattern, working up a swatch a least 10.2 cm x 10.2 cm. If you are getting more stitches per 2.5 cm, then use a larger hook; if you are getting fewer stitches per 2.5 cm than suggested then use a smaller hook. Crochet hook sizes vary by brand and you may be able to find an intermediate size between the standard ones (or a different hook shape or material) that works better for you to get the gauge.

htr = half double crochet

inc = increase, increasing

loop = two or more chains in succession form a "loop"; when working into a loop insert hook below the chains rather than into any single chain.

patt = pattern

rem = remain, remaining

rep = repeat, repeating

RS/WS = Right Side/Wrong Side. Used to designate which side of piece is facing you when working a row or assembling. Usually the WS has a bumpier, less smooth appearance, but not always. Many crochet stitch patterns are reversible or look nice with either side facing, but be sure all pieces match.

skip (sk) = pass over the sts listed after the word "skip". In reading crochet patterns there can be just as much info on what you skip as what you work so that you work into the correct place, therefore you need to read carefully to make sure you understand whether the sts described are ones to skip or ones to execute next.

sl st = slip st

slm = slip marker

space = one or two chains between other sts that form a space; when working into a space insert hook below the chains rather than into any single ch.

st(s) = stitches

t-ch = turning chain, a chain at beginning of a row or rnd that adds the necessary height to start at same level as sts to come.

to within . . . = work until that many sts remain to be worked in the row/rnd below.

tr = treble crochet

turn = turn the piece so that opposite side of fabric is facing ready to work from right to left.

yo = wrap yarn over hook from front to back

ENGLISH/AMERICAN CROCHET TERMS
All stitches here are in English terminology.

READING STITCH SYMBOL DIAGRAMS
The stitch patterns for most of the projects in this book are written out as well as shown in diagrams using universal symbols to represent each stitch. Technical Editor Karen Manthey was instrumental in developing this system of symbolcraft over the past few decades. Her charts practically replicate the crochet fabric and make following the pattern easier. The rows are numbered at the side on which row begins. Use the written instructions to guide you, noting whether you go into a stitch, space, or loop, and where to begin and end if what's shown is a reduced section (repeat) of pattern.

SKILL LEVELS
The projects are graded for difficulty as follows: Easy, Easy Challenge, Intermediate, Intermediate Challenge, Advanced. Don't be afraid to challenge yourself.

RESOURCES

To locate a retailer of the specific yarn used for the projects, contact the manufacturer/U.S. distributor listed below. The company or a yarn shop can help you make a substitution for any discontinued yarn based on the yarn weight, structure and fiber content provided in the instructions. Be sure to purchase enough of a single dye lot to complete the project.

Blue Sky Alpacas, Inc.
P.O. Box 387
St. Francis, MN 55070
888-460-8862
www.blueskyalpacas.com

**Crystal Palace Yarns/
Straw Into Gold, Inc.**
160 23rd Street
Richmond, CA 94804
800-666-7455
www.straw.com

Jade Sapphire Exotic Fibres
148 Germonds Street
West Nyack, NY 10994
866-857-3897
www.jadesapphire.com

Jaeger and Rowan
Distributed by Westminster Fibers
4 Townsend West, Unit 8
Nashua, NH 03063
wfibers@aol.com
www.knitrowan.com

J&P Coats/ Coats & Clark
P.O. Box 12229
Greenville, SC 29612
800-648-1479
www.coatsandclark.com

Knit One Crochet Too
91 Tandberg Trail, Unit 6
Windham, ME 04062
800-357-7646
www.knitonecrochettoo.com

Lana Grossa
Distributed By Unicorn Books
1338 Ross Street
Petaluma, CA 94954
707-762-3362
www.unicornbooks.com

Lanaknits
320 Park Street
Nelson, BC Canada V1L 2G5
888-301-0011
www.hempforknitting.com

Louet Sales
808 Commerce Park Drive
Ogdensburg, NY 13669
613-925-4502
www.louet.com

Mango Moon
412 N. Coast Highway #114
Laguna Beach, CA 92651
949-494-1441
www.mangomoonknits.com

Manos del Uruguay
Distributed by Design Source
P.O. Box 770
Medford, MA 02155
888-566-9970

Morehouse Farm
2 Rock City Road
Milan, NY 12571
866-470-4852
www.morehousefarm.com

Mostly Merino
P.O. Box 878
Putney, VT 05346
802-254-7436
www.mostlymerino.com

Needful Yarns
60 Industrial Parkway
PMB #233
Cheektowaga, NY 14227
866-800-4700
www.needfulyarnsinc.com

Trendsetter Yarns
16745 Saticoy Street #101
Van Nuys, CA 91406
818-780-5497
www.trendsetteryarns.com

NOTIONS

Daytona Trimming
(Cluny lace, rhinestone zippers)
251 West 39th Street
New York, NY 10018
212-354-1713

Greenberg & Hammer
(hooks and eyes, buckles)
24 West 57th Street
New York, NY 10019
800-955-5135
www.greenberg-hammer.com

M&J Trimming
(belt toggle, braided leather cord)
1008 Sixth Avenue
New York, NY 10018
800-9MJ-TRIM
www.mjtrim.com

Purl Patchwork
(fabric, sewing supplies)
137 Sullivan Street
New York, NY 10012
800-597-PURL
www.purlsoho.com

BIBLIOGRAPHY

For the most part I am a self-taught crafter. I've learned crochet by gathering as many books to refer to as possible, trying out established techniques and then experimenting to develop my own style. I've listed some crochet primers below. Plus don't forget to check out the many crochet magazines and online crochet resources. Also note that much of the history of lace-making and crochet has been preserved by Jules and Kaethe Kliot, who founded a publishing and lace-making supply company in the 1960s called Lacis. There is now a museum of their amazing collection in Berkeley, California.

The Harmony Guides: 300 Crochet Stitches. London: Collins & Brown, Ltd., 1998.

Kooler, Donna. *Donna Kooler's Encyclopedia of Crochet.* Little Rock: Leisure Arts, Inc., 2002.

Manthey, Karen, and Susan Brittain. *Crocheting for Dummies.* Indianapolis: Wiley Publishing, Inc., 2004.

Righetti, Maggie. *Crocheting in Plain English.* New York: St. Martin's Press, 1988.

Ronci, Kelli. *Kids Crochet.* New York: Stewart, Tabori & Chang, 2005.

Stoller, Debbie. *Stitch 'N Bitch Crochet: The Happy Hooker.* New York: Workman Publishing Company, 2006.

ACKNOWLEDGMENTS

IT IS A LUXURY TO BE GIVEN THE chance to grow both as an author and as an individual. I view this book as a personal expression embodying my life's work thus far. I tend to take it all too seriously, so it often feels lonely and overwhelming to live up to my own standards and everyone's expectations. Yet, in the process of designing, crocheting, writing, shooting and editing this book, I realized I was not alone but could rely on the talents of everyone involved. I learned that asking for help and deferring to others could be a strength rather than a weakness. Each person's energy and perspective added an essential flavor to make my vision come to life in ways I would've imagined myself if I was truly superhuman.

For providing me with this great opportunity, I must credit my editor, Melanie Falick. Melanie, thanks for carving out a place in publishing's rocky soil where work such as mine can grow organically. An author herself, Melanie is also like the sun, whose light we seedling authors turn toward, striving to reach.

With our second book together, Adrian Buckmaster's photography has become allied to my designs. Somehow our sensibilities are complementary. Adrian, you're brilliant. Thanks for being a true artist. And for treating us all to your homemade vegetarian curry when we shot on your souk-like patio.

We had a great team for the photo shoots. Ally and Kristen Petliski kept us organized. Thanks Kristen for your fresh eyes and coming through with the props, permits, and sexy shoes. Terri Grauel worked hair and makeup magic (and, amazingly, she's the subject of a documentary "The Beauty Academy of Kabul" for the beauty school she started for women in Afghanistan). Several of our models are from Rebecca Kelly company (www. rebeccakellyballet.com) and their dance training brought into play a unique element. Friends and family provided a palette of faces and bodies and lent the garments further character. Thanks go to Aviva, Shamanta, sisters Joy and Jessica, and my own sister Jessica with daughters Haley and Sophia, Ezra, Pearl, Sean, Tod, James, Gumby, Minnie, and Malcolm.

I am indebted to several crocheters who pitched in to make samples—fees alone are never enough to compensate for meeting the challenge. They are Mary Pat Aust, Sara Bennett, Lisa Daehlin, Edie Eckman, Hillary Kolos, Dora Ohrenstein, and Cal Patch. I hope you are thrilled now that you can see your handiwork sewn together and in print.

Ina Braun gave crucial assistance in sample-making, at the photo shoots, and proofreading the patterns. Ina, your sometimes overwhelming enthusiasm and fortitude were, in the end, necessary oil in my creative cogs. You are in a class by yourself. And I guess I am too, but somehow we managed to form a productive working relationship and friendship. May it continue.

I thank Karen Manthey for her technical editing and killer stitch diagrams, Anna Christian for her specialty—book design—and Betty Christiansen for taking on the copy-editing. I also appreciate everyone who works behind the scenes at STC Craft doing whatever it is they do that gets books made.

I wouldn't have been able to work without child care, and so I thank Blanca Maria Ortiz who was Olivia's babysitter for almost three years. We miss you, Mari. I thank my mother and father who continue to parent me much more than should be required at this age.

And I'd like to thank the knitting fans who took my first book to heart and made it a hit. My designs exist in a fantasy world on the page, and it is great to have the luscious images appreciated by a large audience. And it's even more wonderful to see the garments given new incarnations as readers make them. I have met many of you at events and through email and this sense of crafting community has been a surprising benefit of being published. I hope you, like me, are going to see crochet in a new light.